PRAISE FOR THE PREVIOUS EDITION

"One of our world's great problems is egocentric, self-serving leadership—leaders who think people exist for their benefit, instead of vice versa. In stark contrast, Jesus modeled servant leadership, leading by example. He said, 'I came to serve, not to be served.' Now, two thousand years later, Jesus has over 2.1 billion followers, which makes Him the undisputed greatest leader of all time. No one else comes close! This is why you need to know how to lead like Jesus. He is the only flawless example. That's why you should read this book!"

—Rick Warren, Author, *The Purpose Driven Life*
Named One of "America's Twenty-five Best Leaders"
(*U.S. News and World Report*)

"I had the pleasure of hosting at our church one of Ken Blanchard and Phil Hodges's Lead Like Jesus Celebrations. What an impactful day that was for those who participated. I know they will never think about leadership in the same way again. Reading *Lead Like Jesus* will provide you with that kind of experience. Don't miss learning from the greatest leadership role model of all time."

—Bob Russell, Bob Russell Ministries;
Retired Pastor, Southeast Christian Church

"Ever since writing *Leadership by the Book* with Ken Blanchard and Phil Hodges, I've watched them grow in their depth of understanding of what the Bible reveals about how Jesus would have us lead others. The best thinking the Lord has revealed to them, to this point, can be found in this book. If you want to be the servant leader that Jesus mandated His followers to be, then read *Lead Like Jesus*. It will change your life and the lives of people you are able to influence."

—Bill Hybels, Senior Pastor,
Willow Creek Community Church

"You'll find few men better qualified to address this topic than Ken Blanchard. His favorite name is *Jesus* and preferred verb is *lead*. Let him do for you what he's done for me and millions of others—help you lead like Jesus."

—Max Lucado, Minister of Preaching, Oak Hills Church; Bestselling Author

"Finally. Finally. Finally. A definitive guide to the connection between our faith and our work—one that is both theoretically elegant and immensely practical. This is, without a doubt, the most important management book I have ever encountered."

—Patrick Lencioni, Author, *The Five Dysfunctions of a Team*

"Ken Blanchard and Phil Hodges continue to lead us deeper into the gold mines of God's Word to the treasured truth of life. *Lead Like Jesus* promises a refurbishing, applicable perspective from the leader of all time!"

—Dan T. Cathy, President and COO, Chick-fil-A, Inc.

"For those who seek to lead like Jesus, this book is an important reflective tool in helping to better understand—who we are, where we are going, and why it is important for people to follow. It is a reminder to all of us that leadership is only a means. To what end is the ultimate question."

—C. William Pollard, Chairman, Executive Committee,
Billy Graham Evangelistic Association; Former Chairman, ServiceMaster

"There is no greater leadership model than Jesus, and Blanchard and Hodges have taken years of experience identifying the leadership characteristics of Jesus that will affect your life and leadership. They have hit the nail on the head with *Lead Like Jesus*."

—John C. Maxwell, Founder of the John Maxwell Company, the John Maxwell Team, EQUIP, and the John Maxwell Leadership Foundation

"Millions of people wish everyone could lead like Jesus. Ken Blanchard and Phil Hodges have dedicated their time and energy, insights and professionalism, to make it happen. Read this book and ponder the questions raised, the ideas presented, and ask yourself if you too can take up the challenge in your own life. It's not just what would Jesus do, but especially, how would Jesus lead? This book will help you find the answers."

—Laurie Beth Jones, Author, *Jesus, CEO*;
The Path; *Jesus: Life Coach*; and *The Four Elements of Success*

"Ken has a divine passion for leaders to let Jesus live out His life through them in servant leadership. His book, *Lead Like Jesus*, is an extremely timely book that is both thorough and God-honoring. I highly recommend it to all who lead others."

—Henry Blackaby, Author, *Experiencing God*

"*Lead Like Jesus* is a gift to the sincere and a beacon of light to the lost. May the knowledge conveyed in this teaching help spread the message of truth around the world. It has spoken to my heart as well as my mind."

—Mary Anne Shula, Shula Enterprises

"*Lead Like Jesus* transcends all relationships and cuts to the heart of the matter—leading like Jesus will change you and the lives you touch. Choose this book today to be challenged and motivated to lead at a higher level everywhere! You'll never be or lead the same again!"

—Marjorie Dorr, Independent Director, Pharmerica Corporation;
Former Chief Strategy Officer, WellPoint, Inc.

"In *Lead Like Jesus* we learn that it is intimacy with Jesus that transforms our lives and leadership. The difference between this and other leadership books is that the focus on Jesus encourages the leader to actually learn, grow, and change behavior. There is no more effective way to becoming a great leader."

—Vince Siciliano, President and CEO, New Resource Bank

"A path-breaking book in every way. This book shows you how to live your faith in your world—without ducking, without offending. Follow the path and be changed in every way."

—Bob Buford, Author, *Halftime* and
Finishing Well Founder, Leadership Network

LEAD
LIKE JESUS
REVISITED

LEAD
LIKE JESUS

REVISITED

**LESSONS FROM THE GREATEST
LEADERSHIP ROLE MODEL OF ALL TIME**

KEN BLANCHARD
PHIL HODGES
PHYLLIS HENDRY

W PUBLISHING GROUP

AN IMPRINT OF THOMAS NELSON

Published in Nashville, Tennessee, by W Publishing, an imprint of Thomas Nelson.

Thomas Nelson titles may be purchased in bulk for educational, business, fund-raising, or sales promotional use. For information, please e-mail SpecialMarkets@ThomasNelson.com.

Unless otherwise noted, Scripture quotations are taken from the Holy Bible, New International Version®, NIV®. Copyright © 1973, 1978, 1984, 2011 by Biblica, Inc.® Used by permission of Zondervan. All rights reserved worldwide. www.zondervan.com. The "NIV" and "New International Version" are trademarks registered in the United States Patent and Trademark Office by Biblica, Inc.®

Scripture quotations marked ESV are from the ESV® Bible (The Holy Bible, English Standard Version®). Copyright © 2001 by Crossway, a publishing ministry of Good News Publishers. Used by permission. All rights reserved.

Scripture quotations marked KJV are from the King James Version. Public domain.

Scripture quotations marked THE MESSAGE are from The Message. Copyright © by Eugene H. Peterson 1993, 1994, 1995, 1996, 2000, 2001, 2002. Used by permission of Tyndale House Publishers, Inc.

Scripture quotations marked NASB are from New American Standard Bible®. Copyright © 1960, 1962, 1963, 1968, 1971, 1972, 1973, 1975, 1977, 1995 by The Lockman Foundation. Used by permission. (www.Lockman.org)

Scripture quotations marked NLT are from the Holy Bible, New Living Translation. © 1996, 2004, 2007, 2013 by Tyndale House Foundation. Used by permission of Tyndale House Publishers, Inc., Carol Stream, Illinois 60188. All rights reserved.

Scripture quotations marked NKJV are from the New King James Version®. © 1982 by Thomas Nelson. Used by permission. All rights reserved.

Scripture quotations marked PHILLIPS are from The New Testament in Modern English by J. B. Phillips. Copyright © 1960, 1972 J. B. Phillips. Administered by the Archbishops' Council of the Church of England. Used by permission.

Scripture quotations marked RSV are from Revised Standard Version of the Bible. Copyright 1946, 1952, and 1971 National Council of the Churches of Christ in the United States of America. Used by permission. All rights reserved.

Italics in Scripture verses are the authors' emphasis.

ISBN 978-0-7180-7725-9 (TP)

ISBN 978-0-7180-8497-4 (eBook)

Library of Congress Cataloging-in-Publication Data

Library of Congress Control Number: 2015917587

Printed in the United States of America

17 18 19 20   RRD   10 9 8 7 6 5 4 3

CONTENTS

INTRODUCTION

The world is in desperate need of a different leadership role model.
Written a decade ago, the original *Lead Like Jesus* book begins with
this statement, which we believe is still true today.

Our experiences and learnings in the last ten years have continued to remind us that the most important thing in leadership is the
leader; the most important part of the leader is his or her heart; and
the most important connection to a leader's heart is God.

Most leadership resources focus on management techniques,
competencies, strategies, and tactics while ignoring the most
important part of leadership—the leaders themselves. At Lead Like
Jesus, we believe that real, lasting change starts on the inside. When
a leader chooses to allow Jesus to transform him or her from the
inside out, that choice will have an effect on everyone and everything that leader influences. We are clear: you can't lead like Jesus
without Jesus!

A tremendous benefit happens in the lives of people who lead
like Jesus: freedom. Jesus is the only one who offers a model of
leadership that's built on freedom and complete security in Him
and His power at work within us. While the world continues to
throw solutions at us that are built on self-empowerment, self-
reliance, competition, peer pressure, and performance, leading like
Jesus frees us to reach heights of influence we never would be able
to reach on our own. When we are free from pride and fear, free
to humbly accept feedback and admit our mistakes, and strong

enough to overlook offenses and forgive the errors of others, we can lead people and help them reach their full potential.

Still, in the perspective of some leaders, leading like Jesus is "soft" or impractical; for this reason, many leaders continue to bypass it. The results of this way of thinking are clear: continued struggles, dissatisfied employees, frustrated leaders, broken families, split churches, and chaotic, poorly performing teams and organizations.

Try to imagine leaders who lead like Jesus. Leaders who love those they influence so much that they help them get from where they are to where God would have them go. Leaders who hold people accountable, encourage them daily, confront challenges, and bring authenticity, character, and integrity to every interaction. Leaders who want to guide others on the same path. Imagine a world full of those leaders!

There is no need to search further. We have the perfect leadership role model in Jesus. We simply need to follow Him and allow Him to work in us and through us.

Even though we have been declaring for many years that Jesus is the greatest leadership role model of all time, we have not realized the full extent of the leadership gifts He offers us. Jesus is not only the greatest servant leader but also the greatest visionary, the greatest team builder, the greatest team motivator, and the greatest change agent of all time. In fact, we cannot think of any attribute of leadership that Jesus did not model for everyone as He trained His disciples. Now, more than two thousand years later, Jesus still has more followers than any leader the world has ever had.

We have also learned—or relearned—that leading like Jesus is love-based leadership. In fact, God intends the primary outcome of our leadership and influence to be showing people Jesus' love.

Leading like Jesus is essentially a matter of the *heart*. It is also the highest thought of the *head*, it is the principal work of the *hands*, and it is both expressed through and replenished by the *habits*.

The formula *Everything – Love = Nothing* is not of our making. It is the irrefutable law of the kingdom of God, perfectly fulfilled by Jesus. It is also the defining characteristic of the leadership model of Jesus: leading like Jesus means loving like Jesus.

These timeless words of the apostle Paul have much to say to those who are leaders and teachers, who influence the lives of others:

> If we speak with the tongues of men and angels, but do not have love (as our purpose), we have become noisy gongs or clanging cymbals. If we have the gifts of prophecy, and know all mysteries and all knowledge (about how to lead people); and if we have all faith (in our leadership), so as to remove mountains, but do not have love, we are nothing. And if (we engage in selfish acts of self-promotions and) we give all our possessions to feed the poor and if we surrender our bodies to be burned, but do not have love, it profits us nothing. (1 Corinthians 13:1–3, paraphrased)

In this book we will dig deeper into what it means to "love the Lord your God with all your heart and with all your soul and with all your mind" and to "love your neighbor as yourself" (Matthew 22:37–39). We will explore how our formal and informal influence on others can encourage them to develop a closer relationship with God and help them see the love He has for them—the love so beautifully demonstrated through His Son, Jesus.

Included are the following new or expanded lessons we've learned during the past ten years:

- If a leader's heart and motives are not right, all the brightest thinking and most skilled leadership cannot progress beyond the limits of artful, self-serving exploitation and manipulation.
- The Being Habits and the Doing Habits of Jesus provide practical ways to put into action the desire to lead like Jesus.
- Connecting powerful personal testimonies with biblical truths brings added relevance and authenticity to the Lead Like Jesus message for people of different generations and cultures.
- Leadership is about change: initiating change, responding to change, guiding the process of change, reinforcing change, and modeling change for others.
- To lead like Jesus calls for engagement in an interactive personal relationship with God through Jesus Christ and the Holy Spirit.

Ken and Phil are excited that Phyllis Hendry, our dear friend, our sister in Jesus, and the president/CEO of the Lead Like Jesus ministry, is joining us as a coauthor. Her passion for the Lead Like Jesus message and her personal experience of the power of love and leadership greatly enrich this book.

Our prayer is that this book will strengthen your relationship with Jesus and that you will accept Him not only as your Lord and Savior but also as your leadership role model. As you are transformed, people around you will be influenced and drawn to the same model whether they are leading a business, a nonprofit organization, a community initiative, a church, or a family.

No matter how difficult your leadership role may seem, remember what Jesus said: "Come to me, all you who are weary and burdened, and I will give you rest" (Matthew 11:28). Jesus' invitation is still open. And it is open to you.

We invite you to become part of the movement so that someday everyone, everywhere, will be impacted by someone who leads like Jesus.

On the journey with you,

KEN BLANCHARD
PHIL HODGES
PHYLLIS HENDRY

PART I

A BIBLICAL PERSPECTIVE ON LEADERSHIP

Let the peace of Christ rule in your hearts, since as members of one body you were called to peace. And be thankful. Let the message of Christ dwell among you richly as you teach and admonish one another with all wisdom through psalms, hymns, and songs from the Spirit, singing to God with gratitude in your hearts. And whatever you do, whether in word or deed, do it all in the name of the Lord Jesus, giving thanks to God the Father through him.

Colossians 3:15–17

People often see leadership based on an "It's all about me" approach. In all kinds of organizations and institutions, the rewards of money, recognition, and power increase as an individual moves up the hierarchy. Self-promotion (pride) and self-protection (fear) dominate today's leadership style. Many leaders act as if the sheep are there only for the benefit of the shepherd. In personal relationships, leadership based on mutual respect, loving care, self-sacrifice, and openness is often undermined when pride, fear, and indifference replace intimacy with isolation. That's the bad news.

The good news is that there is a better way. This alternative approach to leadership is driven by four basic beliefs that have become central to our ministry:

- Leadership happens anytime we influence the thinking, behavior, or development of another person.
- Jesus is the greatest leadership role model of all time.
- Servant leadership is the only approach to leadership that Jesus validates for His followers.
- Effective leadership begins on the inside, with our hearts.

As you explore these four beliefs, we hope you will gain an entirely different perspective on leadership. May you come to see leadership as a journey that begins with your own transformation and progresses to your leading another person, then to leading a small number of people, and finally to leading an organization. May you also see that leadership is the alignment of four essential domains: the heart, the head, the hands, and the habits.

Let's get started!

ARE YOU A LEADER?

Jesus called [his disciples] together and said, "You know that those who are regarded as rulers of the Gentiles lord it over them, and their high officials exercise authority over them. Not so with you. Instead, whoever wants to become great among you must be your servant, and whoever wants to be first must be slave of all."

Mark 10:42–44

In our Lead Like Jesus workshops, we often ask, "How many of you think of yourselves as a leader?" We are amazed that only about 20 to 25 percent of the people raise their hands, even though our audiences are always predominantly made up of managers and supervisors at every level of a business, an educational institution, a government agency, or a faith-based organization. The reason most people don't raise their hands is they assume that leadership has to do with a workplace position or title. Many people feel they are not high up enough on the organizational chart to say that they are leaders.

We always follow up our first question by asking people to think about the person who has had the most significant impact on their lives, the person who has played a major role in who they are today as human beings. Then we ask, "How many of you named a manager or a supervisor you've worked for over the years?" Hardly a hand goes up. Then we ask, "How many of you identified your father, your mother, a grandmother or grandfather, aunt, uncle, or friend?" Almost every hand in the room goes up. Why is that? Because in reality, every human being is a leader in some part of his or her life—because *leadership is an influence process.* We believe that *anytime you seek to influence the thinking, behavior, or development of someone in your personal or professional life, you are taking on the role of a leader.*

As a result, the only way to avoid leadership is to isolate yourself from the outside world.

Leadership can be as intimate as speaking words of guidance and encouragement to a loved one or as formal as passing instructions along extended lines of communication in an organization. Leadership can be nurturing character and self-worth in children and promoting greater intimacy and fulfillment in personal relationships, or it can involve distributing resources in an organization to reach a specific goal or accomplish a given task.

Thus, there are two types of leadership: life role leadership and organizational leadership.

As a spouse, parent, family member, friend, or citizen, you have multiple life role leadership opportunities every day. What leadership role could be more important than these? Consider some examples:

- a husband and wife who seek mutual agreement on day-to-day finances
- a mother who teaches her toddler how to eat with a spoon
- a son who provides aging parents with advice and guidance about living arrangements

- a person who risks alienation when confronting a friend about a moral failure
- a citizen who helps find housing for the homeless

Different from life role leadership, organizational leadership usually comes with an official position or title that empowers you to serve the perceived needs of an organization. Again, examples might help:

- a corporate executive who rejects offers of insider information that would give his company a competitive edge
- a middle school teacher who excites curiosity in her students
- a rehabilitation nurse who patiently handles a stroke victim's anger
- a pastor who comforts a grieving member of his church
- a high school football coach who focuses more on molding his players' character than on winning games

A key difference between life role leadership and organizational leadership involves the permanence of the relationships involved. Life role leaders function in enduring relationships as parents, spouses, siblings, friends, and citizens; duty and obligation cannot be easily relinquished or discarded.

Organizational leaders, on the other hand, operate for a season in an environment of temporary relationships and fairly constant change. People can come and go very quickly for all sorts of reasons. This lack of stability in organizations often breeds a degree of reserve and qualified commitment evident in competitive office politics.

Most of the significant leadership that shapes our lives does not come from leaders with titles on an organizational chart; it comes from leaders in life role relationships. It is instructive to note that in the early church, a candidate's life role leadership was a prerequisite for assuming organizational leadership. In 1 Timothy 3:1–7 we read this:

> Here is a trustworthy saying: Whoever aspires to be an overseer desires a noble task. Now the overseer is to be above reproach, faithful to his wife, temperate, self-controlled, respectable, hospitable, able to teach, not given to drunkenness, not violent but gentle, not quarrelsome, not a lover of money. He must manage his own family well and see that his children obey him, and he must do so in a manner worthy of full respect. (If anyone does not know how to manage his own family, how can he take care of God's church?) He must not be a recent convert, or he may become conceited and fall under the same judgment as the devil. He must also have a good reputation with outsiders, so that he will not fall into disgrace and into the devil's trap.

One person who exemplified servant leadership in Jesus' life was His mother, Mary: "I am the Lord's servant. . . . May your word to me be fulfilled" (Luke 1:38). She passed on to her Son a legacy of obedience, submission, faith, and service. Mary epitomized the essence of a servant heart. In her life role as a mother, she was positioned to have strategic influence on the life and spirit of her Child. The relationship between mother and Son—between a soul already tested and found willing and a Soul to be nurtured, between a spiritual teacher and a Student—was part of God's plan to prepare Jesus for leadership.

PAUSE AND REFLECT

Take a moment to think about the people who have most influenced your thinking, your behavior, and your life path. As you recall their names and faces, you will realize that leadership titles and positions of organizational authority are only part of the leadership landscape—and usually not the most significant part.

THE GREATEST LEADERSHIP ROLE MODEL OF ALL TIME

"Even the Son of Man did not come to be served, but to serve, and to give his life as a ransom for many."

Mark 10:45

The reality is, all of us are leaders. So, as you lead, who is your role model? We feel the greatest leadership role model of all time is Jesus.

When we tell people this, we get a lot of raised eyebrows. People want to ask what evidence we have—and we're glad when they do.

A few years ago at a Lead Like Jesus teleconference broadcast from Atlanta, Georgia, Ken asked his cohost, the well-known pastor and author John Ortberg, "Why would you travel all the way across the country from your home church in Menlo Park, California, to teach people that Jesus is the greatest leadership role model of all time?"

Ortberg, a gifted storyteller, smiled at the audience and said, "Let's assume for a moment that two thousand years ago you were a gambler. I know a number of you don't like gambling, but bear with me for a moment. Let me ask you, who would you have bet your money on to last: the Roman Empire and the Roman army, or a little Jewish rabbi with twelve inexperienced followers?" Everyone smiled as John went on to say, "Isn't it interesting that all these years later we are still naming kids Matthew, James, Sarah, and Mary, and we call our dogs Nero and Caesar? I rest my case."

While John got a big laugh, his point was well taken. Clearly, Jesus' leadership was effective: His church exists today; the Roman Empire doesn't. Put differently, the important thing about leadership is not what happens when the leader is present, but what happens when the leader is *not* there. As a parent, it's not too difficult to get your children to do what you want them to do when you're hovering over them. But what do they do when you're not there? A business leader deals with the same issue. You can't micromanage your people's every move, much less their every thought or idea. So great business leaders today empower their people to bring their brains to work and make good decisions on their own. When given this opportunity, those people tend to be fully engaged in their work.

Initial proof that Jesus is the greatest leadership role model of all time came to Ken when he was asked to be on Robert Schuller's *Hour of Power* after *The One Minute Manager* was released in the early 1980s. Ken recalls that when Reverend Schuller interviewed him, he asked, "Do you know who the greatest One Minute Manager of all time was?"

Ken gave him a blank stare.

Then Schuller said, "Jesus of Nazareth."

"Really?" said Ken, never having thought of Jesus as a great leadership role model.

"Absolutely," said Reverend Schuller. "After all, He was very clear about goals. Isn't that your first secret—One Minute Goal Setting?"

"Yes," Ken responded.

Schuller then smiled and said, "You and Tom Peters didn't invent management by wandering around. Jesus did. He wandered from one village to another. If He caught someone doing something right, He would praise or heal that person. Isn't that your second secret—One Minute Praising?"

"Yes," said Ken.

"Finally," said Schuller, "if people stepped out of line, Jesus wasn't afraid to redirect their efforts. After all, He threw the money lenders out of the temple. Isn't that what your One Minute Reprimand is all about?"

Ken laughed, realizing Schuller had a point.

This reality was reinforced when Ken learned that Bill Hybels, founding pastor of Willow Creek Community Church, was teaching the leaders on his staff Situational Leadership®,[1] a concept Ken had first developed in the late 1960s with Paul Hersey. When Ken asked Bill why he chose Situational Leadership, Bill was quick to say that Jesus was the greatest situational leader of all time, using "different strokes for different folks" depending on the situation. When, for instance, Jesus first took on His disciples as "fishers of men" (Matthew 4:19 ESV) and sent them out, He provided some specific instructions about where to stay, what to wear, and what to do. But the disciples grew and matured over time: soon they weren't enthusiastic beginners who needed specific direction, and Jesus changed His style accordingly. At the end of His ministry on earth, Jesus was able to issue to His disciples this general directive: "Go and make disciples of all nations" (Matthew 28:19).

As Ken and Phil began to study the Gospels—Matthew, Mark, Luke, and John—as well as the book of Acts, they became fascinated with how Jesus transformed twelve ordinary and unlikely people into the first generation of leaders of a movement that continues to affect the course of world history some two thousand years later.

In fact, Ken and Phil soon realized that every idea and truth about leadership they had ever taught or written came from the Bible and was evident in how Jesus led His disciples.

Followers of Jesus have more in Jesus than just a spiritual leader; we have a practical model of effective leadership for all organizations, for all people, for all situations.

PAUSE AND REFLECT

Have you ever thought of Jesus as a great leadership role model? If not, why not?

JESUS THE SERVANT

"Here is my servant whom I have chosen, the one I love, in whom I delight; I will put my Spirit on him, and he will proclaim justice to the nations."

Matthew 12:18

Having accepted that Jesus is the greatest leadership role model of all time, consider now some specifics about His leadership approach. The best description of Jesus' leadership is found in Matthew 20. John and James's mother had gone to Jesus and essentially asked if, in heaven, one of her sons could sit at His left hand and the other one at His right hand. She obviously thought leadership was all about the hierarchy. After Jesus told her that her request was not for Him to grant, He approached the other ten disciples, who were miffed because this mother had asked for those places of honor before they themselves did!

Jesus called [his disciples] together and said, "You know that the rulers of the Gentiles lord it over them, and their high officials exercise authority over them. *Not so with you.* Instead, whoever wants to become great among you must be your servant, and whoever wants to be first must be your slave—just as the Son of Man did not come to be served, but to serve, and to give his life as a ransom for many." (Matthew 20:25–28)

We added the emphasis on *Not so with you* in that verse. Why? Because Jesus' call to servant leadership is clear and unequivocal. His words leave no room for plan B. He placed no restrictions or limitations of time, place, or situation that would allow us to exempt ourselves from heeding His command. For followers of Jesus, servant leadership is not an option; servant leadership is a mandate. Our servant leadership is to be a living statement of who we are in Jesus, an identity evident in how we treat one another and how we demonstrate the love of Jesus to the whole world. If this kind of leadership sounds like serious business with profound implications, it is.

The exciting part of leading like Jesus is that He never sends us into any situation alone or with a plan that is flawed or sure to fail. Jeremiah 29:11–14 tells us:

"I know the plans I have for you," declares the LORD, "plans to prosper you and not to harm you, plans to give you hope and a future. Then you will call on me and come and pray to me, and I will listen to you. You will seek me and find me when you seek me with all your heart. I will be found by you," declares the LORD.

Whatever subject He addressed—and in Matthew 20 it is leadership—Jesus spoke about what is right and effective. We can trust that His Word is an expression of His unconditional and sacrificial love poured out for our eternal well-being. As followers of Jesus, then, we can trust Him and His instructions to us regardless of our circumstances. We can also freely ask Him to give us wisdom in all things, including our leadership roles. James 1:2–8 reminds us that Jesus wants to be intimately involved in all aspects of our lives:

> When all kinds of trials and temptations crowd into your lives my brothers, *don't resent them as intruders, but welcome them as friends!* Realise that they come to test your faith and to produce in you the quality of endurance. But let the process go on until that endurance is fully developed, and you will find you have become men of mature character with the right sort of independence. And *if, in the process, any of you does not know how to meet any particular problem he has only to ask God—who gives generously to all men without making them feel foolish or guilty— and he may be quite sure that the necessary wisdom will be given him.* But he must ask in sincere faith without secret doubts as to whether he really wants God's help or not. The man who trusts God, but with inward reservations, is like a wave of the sea, carried forward by the wind one moment and driven back the next. That sort of man cannot hope to receive anything from God, and the life of a man of divided loyalty will reveal instability at every turn. (PHILLIPS)

A friend of ours once had a counselor who kept reminding him, "Your intelligence has gotten you into this." You see, in a variety of situations our friend thought he was smart enough to figure it out on his own, but he wasn't. Furthermore, he was trying to gain the approval of various audiences, including some that had conflicting views of what he ought to be doing and how he ought to be living his life. As a result he ended up pleasing no one. He had yet to learn that he had but One as his audience, and that One is God.

In addition to being the only audience that matters, God is also the director of our lives. God will guide us to do exactly the right thing—if we let Him. Our hope is that you will let Him direct you, guide you, and teach you to lead.

IS JESUS A RELEVANT ROLE MODEL FOR US TODAY?

Jesus Christ is the same yesterday and today and forever.

Hebrews 13:8

A common barrier to embracing Jesus as a leadership role model is skepticism about the relevance of His teaching to specific twenty-first-century leadership situations. In many ways, we are in the same kind of situation that Peter was when Jesus asked him to take some highly unusual and unorthodox steps as he conducted his fishing business. Here was the situation as described in Luke 5:1–11:

> One day as Jesus was preaching on the shore of the Sea of Galilee, great crowds pressed in on him to listen to the word of God. He noticed two empty boats at the water's edge, for the fishermen had left them and were washing their nets. Stepping into one of the boats, Jesus asked Simon [Peter], its owner, to push it out into the water. So he sat in the boat and taught the crowds from there.
>
> When he had finished speaking, he said to Simon, "Now go out where it is deeper, and let down your nets to catch some fish."

"Master," Simon replied, "we worked hard all last night and didn't catch a thing. But if you say so, I'll let the nets down again." And this time their nets were so full of fish they began to tear! A shout for help brought their partners in the other boat, and soon both boats were filled with fish and on the verge of sinking.

When Simon Peter realized what had happened, he fell to his knees before Jesus and said, "Oh, Lord, please leave me—I'm too much of a sinner to be around you." For he was awestruck by the number of fish they had caught, as were the others with him. His partners, James and John, the sons of Zebedee, were also amazed.

Jesus replied to Simon, "Don't be afraid! From now on you'll be fishing for people!" And as soon as they landed, they left everything and followed Jesus. (NLT)

What do you think was going through Peter's mind when he replied, "Master, we have been fishing all night and we haven't caught a thing"? It sounds as if Peter might have been thinking something along these lines: *I've listened to Jesus address the crowds and speak with great power and wisdom. I really respect His knowledge of God's Word and His skill as a teacher. But now He has asked me to do something that goes totally against my own knowledge and instincts about how to run my fishing business. Jesus doesn't know fishing; I know fish and fishing. That's my business, and what Jesus asks is not practical. Besides, doing what He says will probably be a waste of time and energy—and my workers are going to wonder if I have lost my mind!*

However, Peter's skepticism did not prevent him from taking the step of faith—the step of obedience—because the instructions had come from Jesus. Because Peter exercised his faith in this way, he experienced miraculous results, but he was overwhelmed by the gap he perceived between himself and what Jesus would require of him.

Jesus sought to calm Peter's doubts and fears, and then He invited Peter to come and be transformed for a higher purpose. And Jesus is issuing the same call to us. Jesus knows fish, and He also knows your business, whether it is in the service of an organization or in a life role.

So consider applying the same criteria to Jesus' knowledge, experience, and success that you would to the hiring of a business consultant. Take a few minutes to think about Jesus' earthly ministry. Would you hire Jesus as your leadership consultant for your life role leadership or organizational leadership positions? Reflect on the following leadership challenges you might be facing and then ask yourself, "Does Jesus have any practical knowledge or relevant experience dealing with leadership issues like these that I face every day?"

- working or living with and caring for imperfect people
- training, developing, and delegating
- being under constant scrutiny by competitors
- continually having your commitment and integrity tested
- handling opposition, criticism, and rejection
- facing conflicting demands from friends and foes
- being tempted by instant gratification, recognition, and misuse of power
- facing serious personnel issues, including turnover and betrayal
- communicating effectively in a multicultural environment
- challenging the status quo and established hierarchy to bring about change
- trying to communicate a radically new vision of the future

- calling attention to poor leadership, even at great personal risk
- putting career or relationships on the line to serve a higher purpose

Chances are, you answered *yes* about every situation. Why? Because Jesus absolutely did face every situation you face. The book of Hebrews says this of Jesus:

> Because he himself suffered when he was tempted, he is able to help those who are being tempted. . . . We do not have a high priest who is unable to empathize with our weaknesses, but we have one who has been tempted in every way, just as we are—yet he did not sin. Let us then approach God's throne of grace with confidence, so that we may receive mercy and find grace to help us in our time of need. (2:18; 4:15–16)

In addition to His leadership experience, Jesus knew from years of personal experience the challenges of daily life and work. Although Jesus was God, He was not ashamed to do a man's work. He spent the first thirty years of His life on earth as a working man: He was a carpenter in Nazareth. Jesus knows the difficulty of making ends meet. He knows the frustration of ill-mannered clients who won't pay their bills. He knows the pressure of meeting deadlines and pleasing customers. He knows the challenges of living in an ordinary home and being part of a big family. He knows the problems that beset us in the everyday world.[1]

Now think about how Jesus would do your job differently than the way you are doing it. As the following scriptures suggest, Jesus wants to do His work in you and through you.

- "I am the vine; you are the branches. If you remain in me and I in you, you will bear much fruit; apart from me you can do nothing" (John 15:5).
- "In the same way, let your light shine before others, that they may see your good deeds and glorify your Father in heaven" (Matthew 5:16).
- "And whatever you do, whether in word or deed, do it all in the name of the Lord Jesus, giving thanks to God the Father through him" (Colossians 3:17).

PAUSE AND REFLECT

If you are skeptical about adopting Jesus as your leadership role model, write down your reasons. What about Jesus is causing you to doubt leading as He leads? And what about *you* is causing you to hold back?

A TRANSFORMATIONAL JOURNEY THAT BEGINS ON THE INSIDE

"Live a life worthy of the Lord and please him in every way:
bearing fruit in every good work, growing in the knowledge
of God."

Colossians 1:10

So you have recognized the ways you are a leader: leadership happens anytime we influence the thinking, behavior, or development of another person. And, aware of Jesus' rich life experience in general and His expert leadership experience in particular, you are willing to follow Him as your leadership role model. The early disciples needed to make that same decision when Jesus extended to them this invitation: "Follow me, and I will make you fishers of men" (Matthew 4:19 ESV). Jesus' simple statement here clearly communicated right at the start that following Him would mean becoming a different person. As they followed Jesus, He would transform them: Jesus would nurture, grow, and refine them. In other words, *leading like Jesus is a transformational journey.* This transformational journey begins with the willingness to do whatever Jesus commands, with a heart surrendered to doing His will, and with the commitment to lead the way He leads.

Transformation happens—for good or bad, to one degree or another—as we interact with people. Your sovereign God will of course oversee that transformation for your good and His glory, and people you lead will be tools He uses in that transformational process. So let's look at who we are leading. As the diagram below illustrates, examining yourself is the first step: this exercise is at the core of leading like Jesus in all of your spheres of influence. You can't lead like Jesus until you accept the fact that only Jesus can lead you. Jesus attested to this truth when He said in John 5:19: "Very truly I tell you, the Son can do nothing by himself; he can do only what he sees his Father doing, because whatever the Father does the Son also does." Think about it: we hear this principle of starting with self every time we hear a safety demonstration on an airplane. The flight attendant tells us to put on our own oxygen masks before we place a mask on someone else. This principle applies in leadership too. Let's look carefully at our spheres of influence.

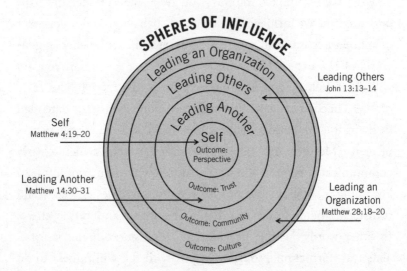

SELF

We believe that leaders who desire to lead like Jesus must first examine themselves by answering these two questions:

1. Whose am I?
2. Who am I?

Your answer to *Whose am I?* defines the ultimate authority and primary audience for your life. Your ultimate authority and most important audience is the one you trust and look to above all else. Your decision about *whose you are* changes everything. If you choose to follow Jesus, you are no longer your own. You are not living to please yourself or other people. Instead, Jesus is the only authority and only audience for every life decision you make.

PAUSE AND REFLECT

Jesus is the perfect example of living for God and for Him alone. After Jesus was baptized but before He began His season of leadership on earth, He was led into the wilderness to be tempted by Satan. There, the evil one tempted Jesus to turn from God's will and instead give in to self-gratification (turning stones into bread), public recognition (jumping off the temple), and the misuse of His power (ruling over all the kingdoms of the world). Each time, Jesus stood strong: He demonstrated submission to His Father and complete commitment to His

Father's way. Jesus knew *whose He was*: "Jesus knew that the Father had put all things under his power, and that he had come from God and was returning to God" (John 13:3). Jesus came from love and knew He would return to love, so He was secure in whose He was.

Knowing whose you are can help you stand strong in your ministry and is foundational to leading like Jesus. Knowing you belong to God gives you the incredible freedom of completely trusting your life to Him. Will you trust God with your life?

The answer to *Who am I?*—the second question that prompts healthy self-examination—defines your identity and life purpose. We are told in Ephesians 2:10 that we are "God's handiwork, created in Christ Jesus to do good works." You were born with a God-given purpose and plan for your life, and you were created perfectly to fulfill that purpose. Your core identity is rooted in the forgiving, saving, and redeeming work Jesus did on your behalf when He hung on the cross. In 2 Corinthians 5:21, we learn that "God made [Jesus] who had no sin to be sin for us, so that in him we might become the righteousness of God." Scripture is full of descriptors of your identity: "dearly loved" (Colossians 3:12), forgiven (Romans 4:7), chosen (John 15:19), "a royal priesthood" (1 Peter 2:9), the apple of God's eye (Psalm 17:8), "the light of the world" (Matthew 5:14), heirs with Jesus (Romans 8:17), friends (John 15:14), and many more. Jesus clearly showed His commitment to His life purpose in Luke 19:10 when He said, "The Son of Man came to seek and to save the lost."

PAUSE AND REFLECT

In what ways would your leadership be different if you truly believed that you are the person God says you are?

Choosing God as your ultimate authority and audience as well as choosing to believe your identity as described in Scripture results in a transformation of your perspective. Your answers to *Whose am I?* and *Who am I?* will change how you see everything, and you will lead others from that new point of view.

LEADING ANOTHER

After leaving the wilderness—after standing on God's Word and resisting Satan's temptations—Jesus called into service those He would lead for the next three years, and He poured His life into training His disciples. Your first test of leading like Jesus will be leading another person. This person may be someone you work with every day, or it may be your child. The desired outcome is a relationship built on trust. Remember in Matthew 14 when Peter jumped out of the boat and began walking on water to join Jesus?

> But when [Peter] saw the strong wind and the waves, he was terrified and began to sink. "Save me, Lord!" he shouted.
> Jesus immediately reached out and grabbed him. "You have so little faith," Jesus said. "Why did you doubt me?" (vv. 30–31 NLT)

Jesus spent three years building a culture of trust with His disciples, including Peter. So when this bold and impulsive follower started to drown, he called out to Jesus for help.

In our life role relationships, trust is the stream by which vulnerability, caring, commitment, and grace flow between parents and children, husbands and wives, brothers and sisters, friends and fellow citizens. Trust is extended first by loving hearts committed to serve and support one another, and trust grows with promises kept, encouragement and appreciation expressed, support and acceptance offered, repentance and apologies received, and reconciliation and restoration established. Yet the stream of trust has a fragile ecological balance: once it is polluted, it will take time and effort to restore it.

The always present power to restore intimacy and broken trust is love. Without love we *are* nothing and we *gain* nothing. Read the following words from the apostle Paul, and ponder the cleansing and healing properties of love:

> If I speak in the tongues of men or of angels, but do not have love, I am only a resounding gong or a clanging cymbal. If I have the gift of prophecy and can fathom all mysteries and all knowledge, and if I have a faith that can move mountains, but do not have love, I am nothing. If I give all I possess to the poor and give over my body to hardship that I may boast, but do not have love, I gain nothing.
>
> Love is patient, love is kind. It does not envy, it does not boast, it is not proud. It does not dishonor others, it is not self-seeking, it is not easily angered, it keeps no record of wrongs. Love does not delight in evil but rejoices with the truth. It always protects, always trusts, always hopes, always perseveres. (1 Corinthians 13:1–7)

PAUSE AND REFLECT

- List three ways you nurture trust as you lead.
- List two things you do that put at risk people's trust in your leadership.
- Think of a time when you lost trust in someone who was leading you. How did you feel? How long did you feel that way? When did you forgive the person—and why?

LEADING OTHERS

The ability to develop and sustain the trust of the people you lead produces community. Jesus modeled this perfectly in John 13:13–14:

> "You call me 'Teacher' and 'Lord,' and rightly so, for that is what I am. Now that I, your Lord and Teacher, have washed your feet, you also should wash one another's feet."

Jesus created a community by empowering His followers to serve and then trusting them to do exactly that. Effective leaders realize they are to be good stewards of the energy and efforts of those they lead; they honor the power of diversity and acknowledge the power of teamwork. As the saying goes, "None of us is as smart as all of us." Jesus sent out His disciples to minister in teams of two (Mark 6:7). In doing so, Jesus empowered them to act on His behalf in support of one another as they accomplished the work He had trained them to do.

Without trust, these relationships cannot be developed, and community will never happen. Individuals in a group will not empower one another to accomplish an assigned task if they do not trust each other. A leader's failure to empower others is one of the key reasons some teams are ineffective.

Family leadership can be really challenging, especially when the leader's efforts and aspirations to serve the best interests of others directly conflict with the leader's own priorities and immediate demands. For example, a father could be running late for work but must stop to make the most of a teachable moment when he hears his daughter ridicule her little brother. The most rewarding results of family leadership are apt to be the subtle fashioning of loving relationships and the slow development of personal character.

Finally, to be good stewards of the efforts of those committed to work with them, effective leaders must honor the power of diversity and acknowledge the power of teamwork.

PAUSE AND REFLECT

How do you think the people you lead at work and at home would describe your leadership in the following situations?

- a time of crisis
- a time of failure
- a time of victory
- a time of plenty
- a time of want

Do you think you would like what you would hear? What weaknesses do you think might be identified—and what might you do to strengthen those traits?

LEADING AN ORGANIZATION

The quality of a leader's influence on a broader organizational level depends on the transformed perspective, trust, and community attained in the leader's first three spheres of influence (self, one person, a small group). Leading like Jesus in an organization creates a new culture that affects all relationships and every result. When people know the leader cares about them and wants to help them grow, a new culture of trust and community develops, resulting in both high performance and great human satisfaction.

By valuing both relationships and results, Jesus created a culture for an effective organization. In His own life, He aligned Himself with the purpose His Father had for Him. Then, in the Great Commandment and the Great Commission, Jesus clearly identified the purpose He had for His followers and their organizations. He equipped His disciples for their work in the first three spheres of influence, and then He sent His Holy Spirit to guide them at the organizational leadership level, a process we see in the book of Acts.

When Jesus called the disciples, He said: "Follow me, and I will make you fishers of men" (Matthew 4:19 ESV). And at the end of His ministry, He said, "All authority in heaven and on earth has been given to me. Therefore go and make disciples of all nations, baptizing them in the name of the Father and of the Son and of the Holy Spirit" (Matthew 28:18–19).

Jesus passed the baton to us. Wherever we live or work, whether we are influencing at home, at church, or in an organization, our paramount task as leaders is to create a culture that reflects Jesus' core value: love. This kind of love shepherds people and organizations from where they are to where God would have them go—and that process usually is not easy!

Leading like Jesus requires leaders to be shepherds and servants, who value each person as an integral part of the organization. These leaders adopt as their core values the principles and practices of Jesus and incorporate those in the organization's training, policies, and systems. When a challenge comes, leaders examine their self-leadership before investigating possible organizational weaknesses.

Joni and Friends, a Christian ministry for people with disabilities and their families, is a perfect example of an organization whose culture has been changed by people who lead like Jesus. Company leaders had no idea what kind of long-term impact this way of leading would have on the organization. What started out as the leadership team's onetime opportunity to learn to lead like Jesus has become an ongoing approach to business that now involves all levels of the organization. Today, Joni and Friends incorporates the concepts of leading like Jesus into every aspect of its operations, including the interview process, new employee training and orientation, and even its conflict resolution policy.

"Leading like Jesus is the cornerstone of our culture," explains Doug Mazza, president and COO of Joni and Friends. "It affects everything we do."

The impact of Lead Like Jesus transformed the organization's culture. "New employees come on board at Joni and Friends, and they are stunned," explains Joni Eareckson Tada, founder and CEO. "They're amazed that we offer Jesus-centered leadership training. It's so unique for any place of business. In every situation, we want our employees to Exalt God Only, and I think leading like Jesus has really helped us infuse that in our culture."

A word of warning: we often think outside the home when we think of an organization. Frankly, no organization is as important as your home. Our life role relationships are based on loyalty and commitment for a lifetime. We can fall into the trap of relying too much on both the resilience of these relationships and our ability to regain lost ground, lost intimacy, and lost love. Life role relationships require daily renewal and nurture; we never know when or how they will end. People in a culture that leads like Jesus will keep their "I love you's" up to date.

Now that we have introduced how to lead in your spheres of influence, let's proceed to the second aspect of leading like Jesus, which provides the framework for the rest of this book: to learn about the four domains of leadership and live out what we learn.

THE FOUR DOMAINS OF LEADING LIKE JESUS

My goal is that they may be encouraged in heart and
united in love, so that they may have the full riches of
complete understanding, in order that they may know the
mystery of God, namely, Christ, in whom are hidden all
the treasures of wisdom and knowledge.

Colossians 2:2–3

The first aspect of leading like Jesus is understanding that such
leadership is a transformational journey. The second aspect of leading like Jesus involves aligning our *hearts, heads, hands,* and *habits.*
When these four leadership domains are aligned, our perspective
is changed, we gain people's trust, communities develop, and the
organization's culture is transformed. When these areas are out of
alignment, our work is unfocused, relationships are broken, communities dissolve, and the organization's culture is unhealthy and
unproductive. The books of Matthew, Mark, Luke, John, and Acts

all offer rich examples of how Jesus functioned in each of these four domains with all of them in alignment.

HEART

Leadership is first a spiritual matter of the *heart*. Whenever you have an opportunity to influence other people's thinking and behavior, you first need to decide whether to act out of self-interest or to benefit those you are leading. Simply put, the heart question is this: Are you a serving leader or a *self*-serving leader?

Whether He was teaching with words (calling His disciples to serve in Matthew 20:25–28) or with actions (washing the disciples' feet in John 13:3–5), Jesus clearly and consistently modeled leadership as service. Identifying the subtleties of our hearts and the veils of justification we place over self-serving motives requires brutal honesty. As John Ortberg wrote in *The Life You've Always Wanted*, "The capacity of the human for duplicity is staggering."[1]

HEAD

The journey to leading like Jesus starts in the *heart* as you consider your motivation. This intent then travels to the internal domain of the *head*, where you examine your beliefs and theories about leading and motivating people. All great leaders have a specific leadership philosophy that defines how they see not only their roles but also their relationships to those they seek to influence. Throughout His season of earthly leadership, Jesus taught and emphasized His point of view. As Jesus said in Mark 10:45, "The Son of Man came not to be served but to serve others and to give his life as a ransom for many" (NLT).

HANDS

You show what is in your *heart* and *head* in what you do with your *hands*: your motivations and beliefs about leadership affect your actions. If you have a serving heart, you will help others reach their greatest potential by establishing clear goals, observing their performance, and following up by praising progress and redirecting any inappropriate behavior.

Jesus poured Himself into His disciples for three years so that when He left His earthly ministry and returned to heaven, they would be fully able to carry out His vision. The principles of establishing clear goals and measuring performance are common concepts for all types of organizations—and are just as relevant and effective in life role leadership relationships. In a family, these principles apply to everything from establishing values and defining guidelines for behavior to describing for a preoccupied teenager what a clean room looks like.

HABITS

Your *habits* are those activities you do in order to stay on track with God and others. Jesus modeled two types of habits for us: Being Habits and Doing Habits. As a leader committed to leading like Jesus, you must make time to replenish your energy and refocus your perspective. Jesus did this through His five Being Habits: solitude, prayer, study of God's Word, the application of Scripture to real life, and supportive relationships—all of which are rooted in and fueled by accepting and abiding in God's love. Jesus expressed obedience to His Father and shared the Father's love for His disciples through His Doing Habits of grace, forgiveness, encouragement, and community.

Since the Being Habits reinforce the good intentions and character of your heart, they will come after the section titled "The Heart of a Great Leader" in this book. Since the Doing Habits reinforce the *hands* aspect of leading like Jesus, they will be described following the section titled "The Hands of a Great Leader." As leaders desiring to lead like Jesus, we are encouraged to engage in both the Being Habits and the Doing Habits.

ARE YOU WILLING TO LEAD LIKE JESUS?

If you understand that leading like Jesus is a transformational journey and if you learn to lead like Jesus in your *heart, head, hands,* and *habits,* your leadership will be radically transformed and its impact magnified. We confidently make this claim not because of any brilliance on our part, but because of the One who is at the center of this effort: Jesus.

PART II

THE HEART OF A GREAT LEADER

Above all else, guard your heart, for everything you do flows
from it.

Proverbs 4:23

Most leadership books and seminars focus on the leader's behavior, style, and methods. They attempt to change leaders from the outside. Yet, as we have taught people to lead like Jesus, we have found that leadership improves when there is first a change on the inside: leadership is primarily a *heart* issue. We believe that if we don't get our hearts right, we simply won't ever lead like Jesus.

What does your heart have to do with leadership? Everything! In the heart is your *why*. Within your heart lies the reason you do what you do; your heart is home to your intention and motivation. It is the core of who you are.

Romans 10:10 helps us understand: "It is with your heart that you believe and are justified, and it is with your mouth that you profess your faith and are saved." It is therefore in your heart that your beliefs about Jesus are stored, and your belief that He is God's Son and your Savior changes everything. As a favorite statement by A. W. Tozer reminds us, "What you believe about God is the most important thing about you."[1]

What we believe about God affects how we deal with life and its challenges, as illustrated in a phone call Phyllis received at the Lead Like Jesus home office. The caller, named Debbie, explained that she worked as a bookkeeper at her church. The night before, she and her husband had been invited to dinner at the home of her boss and his wife.

Debbie said that at one point during dinner, her boss had said, "We're hiring a new church administrator, and he will be doing your job."

Debbie said to Phyllis, "I'm so angry! I've seen other people treated this way at my church. It isn't right, and it isn't fair." She was devastated and furious. She wanted to lash out and give the elders a piece of her mind. Then she asked Phyllis to pray with her.

Phyllis said, "Before we pray, Debbie, may I ask you some questions?"

"Sure," said Debbie.

"Is God good?"

"Yes."

"Do you believe He has a plan and purpose for your life?"

"I *did* believe that."

"Do you believe anyone or anything can change God's plan for you?"

"No."

"Does God love you?"

"Yes."

"Do you believe God will use everything in our lives—that He will use even this—for His glory and our good just as He promised? Do you believe you can trust Him with all the details of your life?"

"Yes."

"Okay. Let's pray."

Have you, like Debbie, faced a challenge so big that you had to go back to the core of what you believe about God? Those beliefs are stored in your heart, and they shape you and every relationship in your life.

PAUSE AND REFLECT

As you reflect on Debbie's story, how would you answer her questions today?

- Is God good?
- Do you believe He has a good plan and purpose for your life?
- Do you believe anyone or anything can change God's plan for you?
- Do you believe God loves you?
- Do you believe God will use everything in your life for His glory and your good just as He promised?
- Can you trust Him with all the details of your life?

As Scripture confirms, the beliefs in your heart set in motion your *why*. In Scripture we learn that the heart is so important in our leadership because love is stored in the heart (1 Peter 1:22). We also forgive one another from the heart (Matthew 18:35); words are banked in our hearts (Luke 6:45); Scripture is stored in our hearts (Psalm 119:11); and it is with the heart that we seek and find God (Jeremiah 29:13). The heart includes the will, determination, and soul. It is the seat of all desires; it is the essence of who we are. No wonder we are told to guard our hearts above all else (Proverbs 4:23).

When leaders want to change, they usually focus on their behavior—but behavior can't change until the heart changes.

Think about your last resolution to diet or exercise. You focused on your behavior: *This time I'm gonna do it!* But nothing changed until you focused on *why* you wanted to make this change. Whatever the specific situation, remembering what motivates you can result in a change of behavior.

A changed heart means a changed leader. Consider this real-life example. Steve Cartin is both a dental practice consultant and a pastor. Initially, he came to Lead Like Jesus for help with his small church in rural South Carolina, but God had more planned for him. As Steve put it, "Learning to lead like Jesus started changing my ministry; then it changed my business; then it changed my relationship with my wife and my relationships with my adult children. By changing me, leading like Jesus changed everything I touch."

The truth is, leading like Jesus begins with the heart.

7

WHAT DOES LEADING LIKE JESUS LOOK LIKE?

Jesus replied: "'Love the Lord your God with all your heart and with all your soul and with all your mind.' This is the first and greatest commandment. And the second is like it: 'Love your neighbor as yourself.'"

Matthew 22:37–39

What does leading like Jesus look like? In a word, *love*—but not the soft and easy kind of love that allows those you lead to do whatever they want, neglects strategic thinking, and fails to focus on results. Of course not! That kind of leadership would be easy, but hardly effective. In contrast, leading like Jesus—leading with love—is very difficult. It requires that you love those you influence so much that you help them move from who they are to who God wants them to be, and that process can be painful. Not often seen in the media, the love we are talking about becomes the core value of your life. It influences everything you say and do as a leader and enables you to stand up when everything else falls down around you.

The greatest description of what love looks like is found in

1 Corinthians 13:4–7, which we shared earlier. This beautiful passage describes God's love and reminds us of what love does and does not do. As leaders who desire to lead like Jesus, we—like Jesus—need the core value of love to be the why, how, and what of all we do.

As a Jesus-like leader, you acknowledge as you lead that God created every person, that He loves them as much as He loves you, and that He has great plans for their lives. As a leader, you need to pour yourself into your relationships with other people just as Jesus did with the disciples. Jesus loved them, served them, and thereby helped them develop into the people God called them to be.

LOVE-BASED LEADERSHIP IN ACTION

Leading like Jesus means that relationships and results are intertwined. It means being committed to both developing others and achieving results in a way that honors God and reflects your core beliefs about whose you are and who you are. We know many business leaders who lead like Jesus in their everyday work lives. One of the first who comes to mind is James Blanchard (no relation to Ken). Throughout his career, Jimmy never saw any separation between faith and work or between being a servant and being a leader. He chose the Bible as his favorite leadership handbook and Jesus as his role model.

For thirty-four years, Jimmy served as chief executive officer of Synovus, a financial services company based in Columbus, Georgia. During his tenure, the company experienced its greatest growth and prosperity. Perhaps even more significant to this discussion, for several years in a row, Synovus was named by *Fortune* magazine as one of the "100 Best Companies to Work For in America." Jimmy is a business guy—a great visionary and skilled strategist who never takes his eyes off the numbers—but he loves people and enjoys helping them grow and develop.

Jimmy always led by serving. "We run our company this way simply because it's right, because every person who works here has great worth and deserves to be treated so," he said. "Our company is built on these values. They define who we are."

In 2005 *US Banker* magazine named Jimmy one of America's "Twenty-Five Most Influential People in Financial Services." He has won numerous awards but believes his greatest award is being married to his wife, Sis, and enjoying their three children and eight grandchildren. Throughout his career, Jimmy has created great relationships and enjoyed great results. God has honored Jimmy for leading and serving from his core value of love.

Jimmy likes to ask people to read 1 Corinthians 13:4–7 and put their names in place of the word *love* in the passage. He often suggests with a smile, "If you notice tightness in your throat in an area, maybe that one needs some work." Jimmy's story is a great example of a business leader living out his faith in corporate America.

A MOTHER'S SELFLESS LOVE

Our next story is an example of a life role leader, a single mom named Karen, who showed incredible tenacity in loving a son who was hard to love. She established boundaries and expectations that were good for him and important for his life, but even as a little boy, Thom pushed the envelope. As he grew, Thom tried everything—he ran away, dropped out of school, lived on the street, and used illegal drugs.

During those years, Karen knew that God loved her son more than she did and that He had a plan for Thom's life. Karen decided that her responsibility was to be a faithful, loving, and prayerful mother.

Thom's behavior continued to spiral downward. One day, after exhausting all other possibilities for helping her son straighten up, Karen swore out a warrant for Thom's arrest for stealing from her home. Karen and Thom lived apart for many years, but gradually things appeared to improve. Unfortunately, the change did not last long, and Thom left his wife and children.

Karen continued to pray for Thom, but she heard from him only sporadically. She repeated the same prayer many times a day: "Lord, I know You love Thom even more than I do. I ask that You protect both his physical body and his heart for You so that someday he might become the man You want him to be. Do whatever it takes to make this change happen—and give me the strength to endure the wait and the pain. In the name of Jesus, amen."

After thirty years, God answered Karen's prayers. Today Thom is the man God intended him to be: he is a devoted husband to his faithful wife and a loving dad to his two daughters.

Leading like Jesus is not just saying, "I will pray for you" or "God will be with you." Leading like Jesus is loving your spouse, your child, or your friend even when that love requires you to stand in the gap. Leading and loving like Jesus requires a vulnerability and an authenticity that close the chasm between saying and doing. It requires holding loved ones accountable while at the same time extending grace and forgiveness.

The rewards of love-based leadership are long-lasting relationships and incredible transformations that bring glory to the One you follow. This kind of leadership requires a model who transforms you as well as those you influence. His name is Jesus.

PAUSE AND REFLECT

The relationships and settings in these stories reflect the core of leading like Jesus: leading with love. In which of your relationships is leading and loving like Jesus a challenge? Continue to think about those relationships as you read this book and consider how to apply what you learn.

8

I WANT TO LEAD LIKE JESUS, BUT MY HEART DOES NOT

I love God's law with all my heart. But there is another power within me that is at war with my mind. This power makes me a slave to the sin that is still within me. Oh, what a miserable person I am! Who will free me from this life that is dominated by sin and death? Thank God! The answer is in Jesus Christ our Lord.

Romans 7:22–25 NLT

You are a leader who truly wants to lead like Jesus, the greatest leadership role model of all time—but you don't. Why?

Paul had the same problem. He articulated his frustration perfectly in Romans 7:15: "I do not understand what I do. For what I want to do I do not do." Does this sound familiar to you?

What is in the heart determines why we do what we do; our hearts are the source of our motivations. What motivates you to lead others? Is your leadership about you? We continue to see that the most persistent barrier to leading like Jesus is a heart motivated by self-interest.

We come into the world focused on ourselves—and some of us never outgrow it. A heart motivated by self-interest looks at life as a "give a little, take a lot" proposition. People with hearts motivated by self-interest put their own agendas, safety, statuses, and gratifications ahead of others'. Cutting people off on the freeway or in the church parking lot, punishing those who disagree with you or challenge your position, and exploiting the weaknesses and fears of others in order to get what you want are actions that come from a heart motivated by self-interest.

YOUR HEART'S EGO—EDGING GOD OUT

The greatest barrier to leading like Jesus is *Edging God Out* of our lives (EGO). We believe you can Edge God Out in three ways: you can replace Him as the object of your worship; as the source of your security, self-worth, and wisdom; and as the audience for and authority over your daily work and life story.

Putting Something in God's Place

You Edge God Out as the object of your worship by putting other things in His place. Whenever anything becomes more important to you than God, that idol becomes your answer to the question, *Whose am I?* You are worshiping something or someone other than God. You may choose to worship an object (money, a house, a car, a business), a person (a spouse or a child), or a desire for power, recognition, or appreciation. A habit that becomes an addiction—exercising, watching sports, eating, sleeping, surfing the Internet—can also Edge God Out and be an idol. You can also find yourself caring most about yourself, your own sense of significance. In Revelation 2:1–7, Jesus called the church at Ephesus to task with the complaint that despite their good deeds and perseverance, they had "forsaken the love [they] had at first" (v. 4). They were no longer passionate about the God they had once worshiped wholeheartedly. Whatever you are worshiping other than God is not worth Edging God Out of your life.

Trusting in Something Other Than God

Another way to Edge God Out is to trust in something other than the character and unconditional love of God as your source of security and self-worth. When you put your sense of security and self-worth in your intellect, your position, your performance, your possessions, or your business and personal contacts, you're counting on things that are temporary and fallible. Instead, place your trust in that which is sure and eternal: God's care for you and the wisdom He provides you.

In his book *The Search for Significance*, Robert S. McGee said, "If Satan had a formula for self-worth it would be: Self-worth equals our performance plus the opinion of others."[1] Yet our performance is not great all the time, and people are fickle; you can't count on their approval. When we seek to build a secure sense of self-worth on the shifting sands of personal performance and the ever-changing opinions of other people, we end up being tossed about in a sea of self-doubt and anxiety. We don't have any security at all.

Valuing Others as the Primary Audience for and Sole Authority over Our Lives

A third way to Edge God Out is to put others in His place as the primary audience for and authority over your daily work and your life story. To whom are you playing from the stage of your life? God wrote your story before the foundation of the world, and you have the privilege of His guidance through all of your life if you let Him be your audience and authority.

One of our favorite old stories beautifully illustrates who our audience should be if we are followers of Jesus. A famous opera singer was invited to give a command performance in a grand theater in front of a large audience. He rehearsed for months. When the night arrived, every seat was filled with fans and admirers. As the singer finished his performance, he was greeted with a standing ovation and made several curtain calls. When he finally came off the stage, his manager embraced and congratulated him. But instead of acknowledging the praise, the singer told his manager that he had failed.

In disbelief, the manager asked, "How can you say that? You received a standing ovation and three curtain calls!"

The singer said, "But a person in the front row wasn't standing or applauding."

"Why do you care about one person's opinion when everyone else loved your performance?" asked the manager.

The singer replied, "The person who wasn't applauding was my teacher."

The singer had wanted to please his teacher above all others. That's how we need to feel about pleasing God.

PAUSE AND REFLECT

Whose praise and affirmation do you seek? Why?

9

THE RESULTS OF A HEART OUT OF ORDER

"A good person produces good things from the treasury of a good heart, and an evil person produces evil things from the treasury of an evil heart."

Matthew 12:35 NLT

EGO PROBLEMS: PRIDE AND FEAR

Edging God Out as the One you worship, as your source of security, self-worth, and wisdom, and as your primary audience results in two EGO problems: pride and fear. When false pride and toxic fear enter a relationship, they poison it. When they become the driving force in your leadership decisions, they render you ineffective.

When leaders are filled with pride or fear, they *react* to things that happen to them. They spend little time considering what is in the best interest of others or their relationships. They shoot from the hip and sometimes end up shooting themselves in the foot. Pride-filled or fear-filled people are quick to judge, quick to

...se, quick to speak, quick to blame, and quick to accept praise.

People who want to lead like Jesus, on the other hand, *respond* to things that happen to them. Before taking action, they choose to step back from the emotion of the moment, even for just a second or two, and, desiring to love and serve, run some value checks on the situation. People who lead like Jesus are quick to listen, slow to judge, slow to become angry, and quick to let someone else receive the praise.

Pride

Pride promotes self. It is *more . . . than* thinking. Anytime you find yourself thinking you are more educated than . . . , better trained than . . . , or superior to . . . in any way, the seed of pride has become lodged in your heart. It can take root, grow, and fully bloom if you allow it. As Paul put it in Romans 12:3, pride is "[thinking] of yourself more highly than you ought," and that is not at all like Jesus.

Here are some of the ways you can tell that pride is at its destructive work. See if any of them seem familiar:

- When you are engaged in a discussion, you resist acknowledging that the other person's idea is actually better than your own.
- You do all the talking, take too much credit, demand all the attention, boast, show off, or, because of your position, demand special treatment and expect better service.
- You judge the value of an idea based on who said it rather than the quality of the thought.
- You treat people as too far below you in position or

credentials by choosing not to seek their input on issues that affect them.

- Your compensation becomes more important as a mark of success than the ethical and relational price you pay to attain it.

The Bible has much to say on the subject of pride. Proverbs 13:10 tells us, "Where there is strife, there is pride." Proverbs 16:18 says, "Pride goes before destruction, a haughty spirit before a fall." And Proverbs 16:5 declares, "The LORD detests all the proud of heart. Be sure of this: They will not go unpunished."

PAUSE AND REFLECT

Identify the last time pride got in the way of your leadership. What action or statement triggered your pride? How did you feel? How did the people around you react to your prideful actions or words? What was the result of your prideful behavior? Invite God to guide your thinking about the situation—and then follow His lead.

Some people reading about pride will say, "Oh, that's not me. I don't have any false pride. I know that everything I am and everything I have comes from God and is on loan to me." Understanding that is great. But often there is a subtler way in which we Edge God Out—fear. Most people don't normally recognize fear as a way to Edge God Out, but fear is at the root of many seemingly prideful behaviors.

Fear

The capacity to experience fear is a gift from God. When heeded, fear protects us. Yet what we actually do with fear when we experience it can prevent us from enjoying the good it can bring. So instead of enhancing life, fear has poisoned human relationships ever since man first stepped outside of God's will. Consider the consequences of Adam and Eve's eating the forbidden fruit: they immediately became self-conscious, covered their nakedness, and hid from God in fear. Human beings have been hiding ever since, because we fear that our weaknesses and bad behavior will be found out. The irony is, God already sees those weaknesses and knows all about our bad behavior.

Still, every day we face the risk of contracting toxic fear—that dark force that can color our relationships and permeate our souls. Toxic fear is a complete anti-God state of mind. It is a good thing turned bad.

In both the Old and New Testaments, the fear of God and the fear of man are held up as the extremes of good and evil. We are called to hold God in life-giving, reverent awe as the ultimate source of our security and judge of our worth. At the end of Ecclesiastes, King Solomon made this definitive statement: "Fear God and keep his commandments, for this is the duty of all mankind" (12:13).

This fear or awe of the holy God is appropriate and even necessary in our faith—and very different from the toxic fear of man. To avoid that toxic fear, we first have to understand its root cause: our addictive dependence on things and others for our security and self-worth.

A good definition of *addiction* is "an ever-increasing desire for something that has an ever-decreasing ability to satisfy."[1] Addictions start as voluntary attempts or choices to experience something desirable, but they end up as compulsions that continually grow stronger and can eventually become completely out of control. When we seek refuge from pain and loss of self-esteem in things like our possessions and our positions, we are vulnerable to having anxiety and fear be key drivers of our thoughts and behaviors.

When something we are addicted to is at risk, toxic fear can poison our daily decisions and relationships in a variety of ways. Here are some examples:

- Rob is a workaholic who is afraid to slow down and look at the condition of his life. He feels trapped when his wife or kids ask for help or when he is forced into a period of inactivity due to illness. He keeps up a schedule of late hours and early mornings to avoid the gnawing feeling of emptiness.

- Janet is a control freak who is afraid of failure, so she chooses personal exhaustion rather than training people and delegating tasks. By micromanaging and keeping other people dependent on her for information, she seeks to protect herself from becoming obsolete or losing her source of power.

- Craig is a fitness addict who goes into an emotional and relational tailspin at the first sign of his own illness or aging—or the illness or aging of someone he identifies with.

- Cynthia is an approval addict who fears rejection and broods over a 2 percent negative rating on a feedback form or an overheard bit of unfavorable gossip.

- Tracy is a sixteen-year-old relationship junkie who will do bad things with bad people rather than face being alone.

Each of these examples of toxic fear is a variation on a central theme: looking for approval from everything and everyone except God.

PAUSE AND REFLECT

Think of a time when the fear of rejection or failure prevented you from doing or saying something that might have helped someone else avoid an impending mistake. What excuse did you tell yourself to justify letting your fear control your inaction? Was yielding to your fear worth the consequences?

THE RESULTS OF PRIDE AND FEAR

It is interesting to see how false pride, fear, and self-doubt play out in organizational leaders. When leaders are addicted to any of these EGO afflictions, their effectiveness drops dramatically.

Leaders dominated by false pride are often called *controllers*. Even when they don't know what they are doing, they have a high need for power and control. They keep insisting they are right, even when it's clear to everyone that they are wrong. They don't want someone else to look capable for fear others might think that person should be the manager. That is why controlling bosses seldom support their people. If everyone is upbeat and confident, the controller puts an end to it. Still, controllers support their bosses more than they support their workplace peers because they want to climb the hierarchy and be part of the boss's crowd.

At the other end of the spectrum are the *do-nothing bosses*, who are often described as "never around," "always avoiding conflict," and "not very helpful." Plagued by fear and self-doubt, these leaders often leave their direct reports alone, even when those people are insecure or don't know what they are doing. Do-nothing bosses don't seem to believe in themselves or trust their own judgment. They value other people's thoughts—especially the thoughts of those with more authority—above their own. As a result, they rarely speak out or support their own people. Under pressure, the do-nothings defer to whoever has the most power.

If any of this makes you squirm a little, don't be alarmed. Most of us have traces of both false pride and self-doubt, because the issue is really the EGO: we Edge God Out as our primary focus in life.

The three primary results of letting our pride and fear Edge God Out of our lives are separation, comparison, and distortion of the truth. Let's look at each of these results.

Separation

Pride and fear always separate us from God, from one another, and even from ourselves. Here are some common examples of the separating power of pride and fear:

Separation from God

We become . . .

- too ashamed about failure to talk to God
- too arrogant to pray
- too afraid of what the answer might be to ask God a question
- too passionate about our own agendas to wait for God to reveal His agenda

Separation from Other People

We become . . .

- too prideful to say we need help or we don't understand
- too fearful of rejection to take a stand on an issue
- too fearful to say *no* when that is the right answer
- too fearful of losing control to share information or power
- too convinced of our own opinions to consider conflicting information

Separation from Ourselves

We become . . .

- too sensitive about other people's opinions to listen to our own hearts
- too busy fixing others' problems to look at the mess inside us
- too ready to make excuses for our failures and unhealthy or unwise choices
- too resistant to introspection
- too obsessed with our own schedules to wait for God's timing

One of the greatest challenges in seeking to lead like Jesus is the intimacy with Him that this approach requires. The biggest barrier to intimacy is a fear of vulnerability—the fear of having to admit you don't know all the answers, that you may need help, and that your abilities as a leader may be questioned. Here, false pride is fear in action.

When you lose intimacy with God and you distance yourself from His unconditional love, you fear intimacy with others. Like the wizard behind the curtain in Oz, you hide behind intimidating false fronts and place barriers around yourself rather than risk exposing your inadequacies and needs. The isolation created by the fear of intimacy leaves leaders vulnerable to being blindsided by changing times and circumstances.

Fear of intimacy can weaken a relationship or an organization like a virus. When this fear enters an organization through the heart and actions of a leader, it is particularly nasty and hard to cure.

Comparison

In addition to causing separation, pride and fear bring about unhealthy horizontal comparisons. Instead of measuring success in terms of how well you are following God's plan for your life, you constantly look around to see how you compare with others, usually on a material basis.

Comparing yourself with others and drawing comfort from feeling superior to others are signs of false pride, insecurity, and fear of inadequacy. Seeking to learn from others and aspiring to emulate good role models are signs of healthy humility. Yet EGO issues and the toxic impact of envy, jealousy, or low self-esteem have been polluting human relationships ever since Cain slew Abel. When leaders foster competition and rivalries among coworkers as a way of driving performance, both performance and relationships suffer. "A little friendly competition" rarely stays little or friendly when the leader makes the rewards for winning too great and the price of failure too high.

When you seek to determine your level of self-worth and security by comparing yourself to others, the end result is either complacency or anxiety. In a larger sense, making comparisons devalues the promises and provisions of God, who has affirmed your value and guaranteed you security based on His unconditional love. You are His beloved.

Distortion

The third result of addiction to false pride and fear is distortion of the truth. The root cause of toxic fear is the lie that we are not safe living God's way and we are going to miss out on something good. We believe the lie because of FEAR—False Evidence Appearing Real. When pride and fear isolate you from everyone else, including God, your view of reality becomes increasingly misguided, and your decisions are more prone to error.

One of the key distortions affecting leader effectiveness is an EGO-driven fixation on short-term results at the expense of long-term integrity. In today's business world, faster access to information brings with it a demand for faster decisions and faster results. Setbacks are less and less tolerated. Annual reports are ancient history; real-time data streams and analysis make quarterly estimates and weekly performance metrics obsolete. Expectations and anxiety built on instant access to data can turn everything into either a crisis or an exhilarating high for an EGO-addicted leader. Direct reports feel as if they have to be on duty 24/7 and immediately inform the boss of any progress.

Jesus spoke of the perils of the distorted and false sense of security and self-worth that comes when we Edge God Out. He said, "Do not store up for yourselves treasures on earth, where moths and vermin destroy, and where thieves break in and steal. But store up for yourselves treasures in heaven, where moths and vermin do not destroy, and where thieves do not break in and steal. For where your treasure is, there your heart will be also" (Matthew 6:19–21).

EGO-driven distortion is also manifested in an overblown view of your ability to control events. When you think and act as if everything depends on you, you're setting yourself and your followers up for failure in the long run. The truth is, as fallible human beings, each of us works within certain limitations. Factors beyond our control and even beyond our awareness can determine success and failure. That fact does not diminish the importance and value of your efforts, but it puts them in perspective, freeing you to extend grace and lead with humility.

This diagram summarizes the concepts of Edging God Out:

EDGING GOD OUT

As the object of my worship	As the source of my security, self-worth, and wisdom	As the audience and authority over my daily work and life story

EXPRESSES ITSELF THROUGH:

PRIDE
An overly high opinion of yourself; exaggerated self-esteem

"Do not think of yourself more highly than you ought" (Romans 12:3).

PROMOTING SELF
• Doing all the talking
• Taking all the credit
• Boasting and showing off
• Demanding all the attention

FEAR
An insecure view of the future, resulting in self-protection

"The fear of human opinion disables" (Proverbs 29:25 THE MESSAGE).

PROTECTING SELF
• Intimidating others
• Hiding behind position
• Withholding information
• Discouraging honest feedback

LEADS TO:

SEPARATION from God, from other people, and from yourself	COMPARISON with others; discontent	DISTORTION of the truth; false sense of security

Now that you understand how your heart Edges God Out and often prevents you from leading like Jesus, we will look at a few of the warning signs of Edging God Out. Let these signs alert you to stop and examine your heart.

PAUSE AND REFLECT

When was the last time you Edged God Out? What was the result?

WARNING SIGNS ON THE PATH TO EDGING GOD OUT

We must pay the most careful attention, therefore, to what
we have heard, so that we do not drift away.

Hebrews 2:1

Warning signs are important: a light on your car's dashboard; the sound of a siren behind you when you are driving; distant thunder before a storm hits. Doctors take your temperature and blood pressure to look for warning signs about the state of your health. We also must check for signs to alert us that our hearts may be out of alignment with God.

What are the warning signs that we may be falling into the trap of pride or fear? And what safeguards can we leaders put in place to prevent this from happening?

WARNING SIGN #1: THE I FACTOR

During a session in which he was receiving counseling, a pastor expressed excitement about his transition to executive pastor of a multisite church. His wife, however, had recently pointed out to him that his tone was curt and his patience was short. She told him his "inner grump" was alive and well. He acknowledged that this was his typical first line of response to challenging circumstances: he was afraid that he was not good enough to do everything the new position required.

His counselor had noticed that, as he was initially describing the situation, almost every sentence he spoke had begun with *I*. The heaviness in his voice indicated he felt great pressure to have all the answers and to not disappoint anyone: "I've got to . . ." "I can't let people down." "I have to work long hours, and my family doesn't understand." The I factor warning sign was there, suggesting that this pastor was depending on himself instead of on God.

PAUSE AND REFLECT

Listen for the I factor in your conversations. Note any words or thoughts that depict you as *less than* (fearful) or *more than* (prideful). Notice whether you too often direct a conversation back to yourself or you interrupt someone's story to tell your own. Are your conversations laced with *I*, *my*, or *me*? Are you others-focused or self-focused? If the latter, consider this a warning sign that you may be on the path to Edging God Out.

A Challenge of Leadership

The following true story tells of an encounter between Abraham Lincoln and one of his army officers.

During the Civil War, President Lincoln was visited by Colonel Scott, a commander of the troops guarding the capital. Scott's wife had drowned in a steamship collision in Chesapeake Bay. He had appealed to regimental command for leave to attend her burial and comfort his children, but he was denied. He took his request to Secretary of War Edwin Stanton, who also refused. In his ultimate appeal, Scott was the last visitor allowed to see Lincoln in the presidential office late on a Saturday night.

As Scott recalled, Lincoln listened to his story and exploded. "Am I to have no rest? Is there no hour or spot when or where I may escape these constant calls? Why do you follow me here with such business as this? Why do you not go to the War Office where they have charge of all matters of papers and transportation?"

Scott told Lincoln of Stanton's refusal. The president replied with equal fervor that, during this time of war, everyone had burdens to bear. He sided with Stanton and denied Scott's request. Lincoln again suggested Scott go to the War Department and if they didn't help him, Scott was to bear his burden until the war was over. Colonel Scott returned to his barrack, brooding.

PAUSE AND REFLECT

Reread the last two paragraphs and notice whether Lincoln's words and suggestions were self-focused or others-focused.

Early the next morning Colonel Scott heard a rap at the door. It was the president. He took Scott's hands and apologized, saying, "I had no right to treat a man with rudeness who has offered his life to his country, much more a man in great affliction. I have had a regretful night and now come to beg your forgiveness." He had arranged with Stanton for Scott to go to his wife's funeral.[1]

PAUSE AND REFLECT

We are prone to making poor decisions when we are **H**ungry, **A**ngry, **L**onely, or **T**ired. So we need to HALT when any of these factors are present.

In the Lincoln case, consider the following:

- What were the internal and external forces that caused Lincoln to first respond in a self-serving way? Note which of the HALT factors might have been present.
- Describe a time when you faced a similar leadership decision. What was your response? Were you a serving leader or a *self*-serving leader? Why?
- What had caused Lincoln to change his mind by the next morning?

WARNING SIGN #2:
THE *MINE* PERSPECTIVE

Have you ever thought, *I would rather do this myself*? Sometimes it seems much easier to do something ourselves than to try to teach someone else to do it. But a critical role for leaders is preparing others to carry on when their own seasons of leadership end. Our leadership legacies are not limited to what we accomplish: they also include what we leave behind in the hearts and minds of the people we work with and teach.

We don't leave much good behind if one of our operating principles is summed up in the word *mine*. The first word of many children is *mine*, and sometimes we don't outgrow that thinking.

Perhaps you haven't thought of your leadership position as a season. But if you reflect on your experience, you probably can see that you have had several seasons of leadership influence in your family, your career, or your volunteer activities. Your personal succession planning efforts speak volumes about your motives as a leader. It is unlikely that anyone involved in the promotion and protection of self—Edging God Out—is going to spend much time training and developing a potential successor. One mark of EGO-driven leaders is this failure to groom someone to take their place. Also limiting the development of those we lead are such behaviors as hoarding information, refusing to empower coworkers to make decisions, and failing to recognize people's contributions.

During His time on earth, Jesus modeled a sacrificial passion for ensuring that His followers were equipped to carry on the movement He had begun. Jesus lived in intimate relationship with the very people He wished to empower by His words and example. In his book *Transforming Leadership*, author Leighton Ford notes, "Long before modern managers, Jesus was busy preparing people for the future. He wasn't aiming to pick a crown prince, but to create a successor generation. When the time came for Him to leave, He did not put in a crash program of leadership development—the curriculum had been taught for three years in a living classroom."[2]

Whom are you developing in your living classroom?

WARNING SIGN #3:
NEGATIVE RESPONSE TO FEEDBACK

Do you appreciate feedback? When we ask that question, most people say, "Yes, but . . ." We hear, "Yes, but not from someone I don't respect" or "Yes, but only from certain people."

Maybe you often receive feedback graciously, but in some situations it may not be helpful or it may be out of alignment with your purpose and mission. Everyone likes positive feedback, but you may have a difficult time with negative feedback—especially if your security and self-worth are based on public image, reputation, position, competitive performance, possessions, or personal relationships. If you sense a threat to any of those things you cherish, you may react to criticism in a fearful, defensive way. You may also wrongly conclude that negative feedback means people don't want you to lead anymore. That's not always the case. Sometimes the biggest fear is not failure; it is the fear of losing your power and position. The fear is intensified if you have based your self-worth and security on your leadership position and power.

With some honest self-evaluation, you may come to realize that you, too, have an EGO problem. That's the bad news. The good news is twofold: you are not alone, and what you are struggling with is a treatable condition. In 1 Corinthians 10:13 we read:

No temptation has overtaken you except what is common to mankind. And God is faithful; he will not let you be tempted beyond what you can bear. But when you are tempted, he will also provide a way out so that you can endure it.

In his classic book *Ordering Your Private World*, Gordon MacDonald says there are two types of people in the world: *driven* people and *called* people.[3]

Driven people think they own everything. They own their relationships, they own their possessions, and they own their positions. In fact, they perceive their identity as the sum of their relationships, possessions, and positions. As a result, driven people spend most of their time protecting what they own. We see this in a family when a father or mother demands that everyone cater to his or her wishes without questioning that person's authority. Driven people believe "the one who dies with the most toys wins"—and if you mess with any of their toys, you're in trouble. The possessions of driven people become an important expression of who they are, and sometimes their possessions end up possessing them.

Called people, on the other hand, believe everything they have is on loan to them from the Lord. They believe, for instance, that their relationships are on loan and are to be cherished; they know there is no guarantee they will see those they love tomorrow. Called people also believe their possessions are on loan and are to be held lightly, to be enjoyed and shared with an open hand. Finally, called people believe their positions are on loan from God, as are the people they are leading and influencing. Rather than protecting what they own, called leaders act as good stewards of the resources and people who have been loaned to them. They are therefore prone to see feedback as more of a gift than a threat. Even if feedback is hurtful or given in a negative way, leaders grounded in God's unconditional love will move beyond the negative emotions and seek to find truth that will help them improve their leadership.

PAUSE AND REFLECT

Have these warning signs helped you diagnose a heart problem? The first step toward wellness is admitting that you are Edging God Out with pride or fear. Ask yourself these questions:

- When you consider the I factor, do you Edge God Out more because of fear or pride? Give specific evidence.

- Have you overcome your *mine* perspective? Be honest and offer specifics.
- What is your first reaction when somebody criticizes you or disagrees with your decision? Why? Do you become defensive? If so, why?
- In your positions of leadership, do you have feedback rules? Who can give you feedback? When can they give you feedback? And do those you're leading know these rules?
- What do your answers to these questions show you about your leadership?

A HEART TURNAROUND

Jesus said to his disciples, "Whoever wants to be my disciple must deny themselves and take up their cross and follow me."

Matthew 16:24

Leading like Jesus is not easy. It demands intentionality and commitment as well as an ongoing relationship with the model you are trying to follow. Frankly, it can be easy to lose focus due to hectic schedules and great demands on your time. The temptation to put something else in God's place—to choose another source of security, self-worth, or wisdom and another audience and authority for your life—is constant. A life intentionally lived with a focus on Jesus and a deep commitment to Him will help you move from Edging God Out to Exalting God Only.

CHOOSE GOD AS THE OBJECT OF YOUR WORSHIP

We know we should place God above everything else, but we don't always do so. Ensuring God is in His right place and you are in yours is always a heart issue.

Adam and Eve thought they knew better than God and became

the first people to Edge God Out. Your beliefs about God are stored in your heart, but shiny things can pull you away. We can too easily fall into worshiping, for instance, success, power, money, family, education, reputation, and good works, instead of God.

Only when you really know God will He truly be the object of your worship. When you know God is good, when you know He loves you with no strings attached, and when you know that He will never leave you, then you can trust Him above all others and you will worship Him more freely. When you are in deep trouble and the only One you can call on is your heavenly Father—the One who put the stars in place, who loved you first, who created you, and who has a perfect plan for your life—then you will worship Him more wholeheartedly. We come to know God through our experiences with Him, and our worship of God increases and is enriched as we come to know Him better.

PAUSE AND REFLECT

Think about a time in your life that seemed hopeless. Maybe you experienced the death of someone you loved, a divorce, a job loss, or separation from friends or family. We often come to know God in a deeper way when we experience Him in the hard moments of our lives.

Now think about a time when life was so good that you couldn't find words to express your gratitude. Maybe the blessing was the birth of a child or grandchild, a promotion you worked toward for a long time, or your child's marriage to a wonderful, God-honoring person. Knowing God better also happens as our gratitude at seeing His goodness overflows.

Finally, when did you experience a time when you tried to find things and people to fill you up, but your tank stayed empty? Knowing God better happens when you learn that nothing can truly satisfy you except a relationship with Jesus.

Scripture reminds us:

His divine power has given us everything we need for a godly life through our knowledge of him who called us by his own glory and goodness. Through these he has given us his very great and precious promises. (2 Peter 1:3–4)

As Peter proclaimed, God has given us everything we need for living a godly life, a life of worshiping Him more fully as we come to know Him better. So if we want to lead like Jesus, we will be intentionally focused on knowing God. This intimate knowing will prompt us and enable us to worship Him with our lives as we spend time with our families, at work, or serving at church or in the community.

CHOOSE GOD AS THE SOURCE OF YOUR SECURITY, SELF-WORTH, AND WISDOM

Choosing God as the source of all you need changes your perspective, your purpose, and your goals. Believing that your security and self-worth are not up for grabs every day and that He will give you wisdom in every moment of your life brings peace and freedom.

Everyone wants to feel secure in this world of uncertainty. You have a sense of how your life will unfold; you think you know pretty much what it will look like. But then something changes—your spouse wants a divorce, you lose your job, or you are diagnosed with a life-changing or life-threatening disease—and you have to reframe your ideas and expectations. You will no longer feel secure unless the source of your security is God. When you Exalt God Only, you answer the question *Can I trust God?* with a definite *yes*. You have come to know Him intimately, and you know you can trust Him no matter what the circumstances of your life. God is the source of your security, and He will never fail you.

PAUSE AND REFLECT

Psalm 20:7 says, "Some trust in chariots and some in horses, but we trust in the name of the LORD our God." Where do you place your trust?

Self-worth is not just feeling good about yourself; it comes from a healthy sense of your identity and purpose. When you Exalt God Only, you are mindful that you belong to God. You trust Him with your life, and you trust that you are who God says you are. You find your purpose and identity in Him: you are beloved, forgiven, righteous, holy, acceptable, and more. Your purpose is sure because you trust God to keep the promises made in Scripture. Ephesians 2:10 reads: "We are God's masterpiece. He has created us anew in Christ Jesus, so we can do the good things he planned for us long ago" (NLT). When God is the source of your self-worth, you are no longer imprisoned by the pressure to do more and try harder. You can actually be a human *being*, not a human *doing*, and you can relax in who God has made you to be. In doing so, you exalt God.

Choosing God to be the source of your wisdom means you are no longer focused on the world's view. You have a different perspective and set of priorities. Scripture says you have the mind of Christ, and you recognize the Bible as the only playbook for your life. When you Exalt God Only, you are focused on Him: you lean in to Him in order to hear His wise counsel. You have come to trust God enough to wait for His answers. You understand that in the waiting, He is growing you to trust Him more.

Jesus is the supreme example of how to depend on God the Father as your source for everything—including self-esteem and security. Jesus said:

> "The Son can do nothing by himself; he can do only what he sees his Father doing, because whatever the Father does the Son also does. For the Father loves the Son and shows him all he does. Yes, and he will show him even greater works than these, so that you will be amazed. . . . By myself I can do nothing; I judge only as I hear, and my judgment is just, for I seek not to please myself but him who sent me." (John 5:19–20, 30)

CHOOSE GOD AS THE AUDIENCE FOR AND AUTHORITY OVER YOUR DAILY WORK AND LIFE STORY

Choosing God as your audience means that your eyes are on God, not on people. He is your Audience of One; like you, everyone else is a member of the cast. The scribes and Pharisees of Jesus' day didn't play to the Audience of One, however, and Jesus was scathing in His judgment of them. He called them hypocrites because they did their good deeds to be seen by men:

> "Everything they do is done for people to see. . . . They love the place of honor at banquets and the most important seats in the synagogues; they love to be greeted with respect in the market-places and to be called 'Rabbi' by others." (Matthew 23:5–7)

When you choose God as the authority for your life, obedience to His Word is your standard. The first step in living out this choice is to return to Him the love He has shown us, and that means obeying Him. Jesus put it this way: "Anyone who loves me will obey my teaching. My Father will love them, and we will come to them and make our home with them" (John 14:23). Now, that is a great deal!

Our obedience is born out of our love of God. We Exalt God Only when we choose to live in His love. That choice is easier when we remember that God has already chosen us and, through Jesus, made Himself and His love known to us. Exalting God happens when we understand that Jesus is the gift that becomes our audience and authority.

RESULTS OF EXALTING GOD ONLY: HUMILITY AND CONFIDENCE

If God is the object of your worship, the source of your security and self-worth, and your audience and authority, then humility and God-grounded confidence will replace false pride and fear. Instead of Edging God Out because we are driven by pride and fear, our relationships and leadership will be renewed with humility and God-grounded confidence as we seek to Exalt God Only. The challenge is first to understand the nature of the journey we must travel and then to commit to taking the initial steps.

Humility

Leading like Jesus means leading with humility, the first attribute of a heart that Exalts God Only. Humility requires knowing *whose you are* and *who you are*. You are called to be a good steward of your season of influence, remembering there is a plan that was set in motion long before you were born. By God's grace, your influence will extend beyond your tenure in the hearts and minds of those the Lord entrusted to your care.

> Do not think of yourself more highly than you ought, but rather think of yourself with sober judgment, in accordance with the faith God has distributed to each of you. (Romans 12:3)

As a leadership trait, humility is a heart attitude that reflects a keen understanding of your limitations and even inability to accomplish something on your own. When a victory is won or an obstacle overcome, humility gives credit to people and forces other than your own knowledge and effort. According to Jim Collins in his book *Good to Great*, a leader with a humble heart looks out the window to find and applaud the true causes of success and in the mirror to find and accept responsibility for failure.[1] A leader who does that is not suffering from low self-esteem! In fact, as Ken and Norman Vincent Peale said, "People with humility don't think less of themselves; they just think of themselves less."[2]

Leading like Jesus also requires humbly accepting and honoring the nonnegotiable boundaries He has set so you can accomplish true and lasting results. Jesus said to His disciples, "I am the vine; you are the branches. If you remain in me and I in you, you will bear much fruit; apart from me you can do nothing" (John 15:5).

There is, however, a difference between putting on the appearance of humility before others and being truly humble in the presence and before the purposes of God. You are not to be piously humble about what He has given you or what you have done. In *Breakfast with Fred*, Fred Smith said it well: "People with humility don't deny their power; they just recognize it passes through them, not from them."[3]

Humility is realizing and emphasizing the importance of other people. It is not putting yourself down; it is lifting others up. It is saying to yourself and to others, "I am precious in God's sight—and so are you."

The humility Jesus demonstrated did not rise from a lack of self-esteem, love, power, or ability. His humility came from the fact that He knew whose He was, who He was, where He came from, and where He was going. That understanding freed Him to treat people with love and respect.

God-Grounded Confidence

Humility rooted in a secure relationship with His Father allowed Jesus to approach every situation with God-grounded confidence, the second attribute of a heart that Exalts God Only. Jesus always knew His Father unconditionally loved Him. That gave Him confidence to stay focused on the reason He had come to earth.

Minister and author Norman Vincent Peale often said the toughest test of self-esteem is bowing your head, admitting to

God that you fall short of perfection, and accepting Jesus as your Savior. Norman told Ken that at times people would say to him, "Christianity is for weaklings." Norman said when that happened, he would reply, "That's furthest from the truth. The human EGO does not want to admit any weakness." Moving from self-confidence to God-grounded confidence takes a big person and an even bigger, loving God.

One of the by-products of God-grounded confidence is the "peace of God, which transcends all understanding" (Philippians 4:7). Jesus promises to give us this peace when we surrender our lives to Him: "Peace I leave with you; my peace I give you. I do not give to you as the world gives. Do not let your hearts be troubled and do not be afraid" (John 14:27).

Clearly, Exalting God Only will make you a different kind of leader. Humility and God-confidence will mark your leadership and have an impact on those you influence. Pride and fear no longer hold you captive: you don't have to prove anything to anyone, and you can rest in knowing and worshiping God, trusting Him as your source, your audience, and your authority. Jesus came to set the captives free, and freedom comes when we give ourselves totally to God and exalt Him only.

When we Exalt God Only, our perspectives change. Edging God Out separates us from God, from others, and from ourselves; prompts us to compare ourselves to others; and offers only a false sense of security. But when we Exalt God Only, we move toward community and transparent relationships rather than toward separation and isolation; from comparisons of ourselves to others to contentment with whose we are and who we are; and from distorted thinking about God and about ourselves to the truth of God's love for us as a basis of decision making and leading.

EXALTING GOD ONLY

| As the object of my worship | As the source of my security, self-worth, and wisdom | As the audience and judge of my life decisions |

EXPRESSES ITSELF THROUGH:

HUMILITY

Something to hope for but never claim; something to observe in others

"Do nothing out of selfish ambition or vain conceit. Rather, in humility value others above yourselves" (Philippians 2:3).

Looking out the window, not in the mirror, to praise

A kingdom perspective

GOD-GROUNDED CONFIDENCE

Resting assured in God's nature and goodness; proceeding in faith one step at a time

"So we can confidently say, 'The Lord is my helper; I will not fear; what can man do to me?'" (Hebrews 13:6 ESV).

Promoting others

Protecting others

LEADS TO:

| COMMUNITY Drawing near to God and to others | CONTENTMENT Being satisfied in all circumstances | TRUTH as a basis for decision making |

PAUSE AND REFLECT

Imagine sitting down with Jesus just before He sends you off to represent His kingdom where you work and in all your personal relationships. Here are some questions Jesus might ask to make sure you are ready to head out:

- Do you love Me?
- Do you trust Me?
- Will you serve Me by serving others?
- Do you believe that I will always love you regardless of your performance or the opinions of others?
- Are you willing to set aside recognition, power, and instant gratification to honor Me by doing the right thing?

PART III

THE BEING HABITS

Though you have not seen him, you love him; and even though you do not see him now, you believe in him and are filled with an inexpressible and glorious joy, for you are receiving the end result of your faith, the salvation of your souls.

1 Peter 1:8–9

How can you Exalt God Only? It seems so easy for other things, people, or circumstances to crowd out your priorities and take over as the object of your worship. When the world so loudly and persistently shouts out its promises, what can you do to better rely on God as your source of security, self-worth, and wisdom and to more consistently choose Him as your audience and authority?

You have heard messages since you were a child about what it takes to be a success—whatever *success* means in a given context. You have been bombarded with commercials and social media messages that define for you the right career, the right kind of car, the right look, power positions, success, and the home of your dreams. What can you possibly do to guard your heart and exalt God when the pull to choose differently is so strong?

As Jesus moved through His season of earthly leadership, He experienced constant pressure and ongoing temptation to stray from the path God had set out for Him. We learn a lot by reading in Scripture what Jesus did to stay on track with His mission. We find five key *Being Habits* that countered the negative forces in His life; habits that we ourselves can adopt.

You'll notice that the central habit is accepting and abiding in God's love. The other four habits—experiencing solitude, practicing prayer, knowing and applying Scripture, and maintaining supportive relationships—are all ways to help you accept and abide in God's unconditional love.

Adopting these habits is essential for those of us who seek to follow Jesus as our role model for leadership. He led with these five habits—and if we want to lead like Jesus, we will too.

Why are these habits essential?

Practicing the Being Habits gives you peace. If peace sounds like a strange characteristic for a leader, think about how Jesus, the

Prince of Peace, exhibited it throughout His ministry. Peace is an attractive trait in a leader, and many leaders rise to power on their promises of peace. Jesus knew peace in His Father, and He lived out peace even when everything around Him seemed in conflict or chaos. When people sense a leader's solid self-control, they have greater faith in what he or she is doing.

As Rick Warren observed in *The Purpose Driven Life*, "Your character is essentially the sum of your habits."[1] So if we want to develop a character like Jesus', we have to look carefully at His habits. And if we want to become more like Jesus, there is only one way: choose to set aside time to be with God.

You may spend this time in solitude, prayer, or the study of Scripture, but the focus of your time with God is to nourish, strengthen, and grow your relationship with Him. Your time with God will help you get to know Him better and to understand more fully His love for you. Your choice to be in close relationship with God is the one choice that both transforms you and consequently affects everyone around you.

Furthermore, the truth is that you can't keep your heart in its right place by yourself. The One who created you for His great purpose, who loves you more than anyone else does, who knew your last day before your first day began, is the One who calls you to be with Him. It is in being with Him that you become more the person God created you to be: you become more like Jesus.

12

THE HABIT OF ACCEPTING AND ABIDING IN GOD'S UNCONDITIONAL LOVE

We know and rely on the love God has for us. God is love.
Whoever lives in love lives in God, and God in them.

1 John 4:16

It is hard to imagine that the God of the universe actually seeks a love relationship with you and me. It is hard to imagine because we know ourselves all too well. We know what we are capable of: we know we can be prideful, fearful, mean-spirited, and worse. And we understand conditional relationships, but this powerful love with no strings attached is hard to comprehend. Ephesians 3:17–19 says:

Christ will make his home in your hearts as you trust in him.
Your roots will grow down into God's love and keep you strong.
And may you have the power to understand, as all God's people
should, how wide, how long, how high, and how deep his love is.
May you experience the love of Christ, though it is too great to

understand fully. Then you will be made complete with all the fullness of life and power that comes from God. (NLT)

What a promise! Your relationship with Jesus is built on the truth that we love because He first loved us (1 John 4:19). When you choose to set aside time to be with God, you will come to know Him better, the foundation of your relationship with Him will grow stronger, and you can come to more fully accept and more completely abide in His unconditional love.

There are not, however, four or five easy steps to accepting and abiding in God's love. This habit has nothing to do with how many times you attend church in a month, how often you pray each day, how much money you give to missions, or how many business deals you complete in a week. This habit has nothing to do with your success as a parent, pastor, or business leader. God's love is a gift. Accepting and abiding in His love requires the foundational belief that His love for you is possible. Believing that it is possible for God to love you will lead you to Him—and He enables us to believe He loves us by His Son's death on the cross and His Holy Spirit's work in our hearts.

PAUSE AND REFLECT

Think of a time when you felt loved by God. What were the circumstances? Were you alone with God, in a group, listening to music, reading Scripture, seeing your child walk for the first time, opening your new business, or watching a sunrise?

What steps could you take to feel His love now? One step is simply to ask your heavenly Father to reveal His love to you.

Love draws us into relationships. In fact, you and I are most often drawn to people who love us, especially those who love us not because of what we do for them, but because of who we are. Maybe you have experienced a child or grandchild running to meet you with open arms. There is tremendous joy in the open arms of a child who loves you.

Phyllis recently had an experience in a fast-food restaurant that reminded her of what it is to love without conditions. She was walking toward the drink machine and saw a little girl of about three waiting while her dad filled their cups. The girl saw Phyllis and ran to her, smiling, and Phyllis smiled back. The girl's dad walked over and explained that his daughter had never run up to a stranger that way before. Phyllis said she must look like someone the girl knows. The little girl walked away with her dad but then turned and ran back to Phyllis, this time wrapping her arms around Phyllis's legs. Surprised, her dad came back and apologized, saying he had no idea what would make the girl behave like this. He picked her up and carried her off. Phyllis felt blessed to be the proxy for whomever the little girl loved so much. The experience felt like a gift to her after a very long day. She chose to believe God sent a little child to remind her of His love for her.

Perhaps the greatest earthly picture of unconditional love is a parent's love for a child. At our seminars, when we ask parents to raise their hands if they love their kids, all the hands go up. When we ask how many of them love their kids only if they're successful, all the hands go down. You love your kids unconditionally, right? But some human relationships have taught us about conditional love and left us broken and wounded. This experience can color our relationship with our heavenly Father.

God's love, however, is not like any other love. Read the following promises of God and personalize them by inserting your name in the blank.

- _____, I know you by name.
- _____, I have loved you with an everlasting love.
- _____, I gave My life for you.
- _____, I have great plans for you.
- _____, nothing can separate you from My love.
- _____, I will wipe away every tear from your eyes.
- _____, ask and you will receive.
- _____, I want you to have life and have it to the full.
- _____, I take great delight in you.
- _____, I am with you wherever you go.
- _____, I will never leave you nor forsake you.

We live in a world that fuels pride and fear. Through fads, fashion, and societal pressure to acquire more, we are lured into believing we can secure for ourselves a sense of meaning and safety. In absolute contrast to these temporary, always-at-risk places to put our trust are the unconditional love and never-failing promises of God. Only in relationship with God can we find and be assured of a never-ending supply of what we need to live and lead like Jesus.

Knowing God's love for you offers assurance of whose you are and who you are. You are God's—His chosen, who is beloved, forgiven, righteous, and more. Accepting and abiding in God's love means recognizing that every gift you have is a gift from God. No pride can exist in the face of such grace and generosity, and no fear can grab you from the safety of His unconditional love.

If God's love for you were based on your performance—on how well you lived up to His standards of righteousness—you would never be free of anxiety. The alternative is to accept God's unconditional love for you: admit that you can't earn enough, achieve enough, or control enough to get any more love from Him. In Jesus you already have access to all the love you need and infinitely more.

That truth is so powerful. Once you believe that you are completely and unconditionally loved by God, you won't be misled by earthly things that offer love, peace, safety, and security.

Accepting and abiding in God's love, though, is not a onetime decision. It is a habit to be practiced, day by day, hour by hour, even minute by minute. When the world tells you that you are not enough, when fear paralyzes you because failure seems imminent and inevitable, the habit of accepting and abiding in God's love will help you remember that you are unconditionally loved. Soak in those scriptures that remind you of God's love, listen to music that reinforces God's love, and spend time with people who share God's love with you. Whatever it takes to anchor that understanding in your heart, do it.

You will be able to lead like Jesus only if you have received the gift of God's love. His love for us is the foundation of our Jesus-like leadership. We cannot give to others love, peace, hope, or security if we ourselves have not received it first.

You might be thinking, *Why are you talking about accepting and abiding in God's unconditional love in a book on leadership?* Good question. The answer is this: God's love will change you and, by extension, change your leadership. You will see leadership differently: it becomes less about power and control and more about the stewardship of the people you touch and of the work God has given you to do. You will see people differently, too: rather than seeing them as a means to accomplish the results you want, you realize that God has the same love for them that He has for you. Work becomes an act of worship and your workplace an outpost of God's kingdom. You are no longer threatened by feedback; you no longer lead out of fear or cause others to be fearful of you. Accepting and abiding in God's unconditional love changes you and lays the foundation for the four other Being Habits that will help you lead like Jesus.

PAUSE AND REFLECT

At the beginning of this chapter, we said it is hard to imagine that God could love us unconditionally because we know ourselves. Pause for just a few minutes, put your doubts aside, and imagine fully embracing the truth that you are unconditionally loved by Almighty God. Accept that you can't earn that kind of love, you don't deserve it, and you can't add to it or lose it. What in your life would you be doing differently if you lived with absolute confidence in God's love for you?

Now think of a time when, beyond a shadow of doubt, you experienced God's unconditional love for you so personally and specifically that only He and you knew the moment's true significance. How did you feel at the time? How do you feel now as you think back on that moment? What do you want to say to God?

13

THE HABIT OF EXPERIENCING SOLITUDE

> Very early in the morning, while it was still dark, Jesus got up, left the house and went off to a solitary place, where he prayed.
>
> Mark 1:35

Of the habits we are going to discuss, solitude is by far the most elusive in our modern world of noise, busyness, and 24/7 communications. Solitude is truly countercultural and therefore a challenging behavior to adopt. Furthermore, solitude draws us into the very place so many of our activities seem designed to help us escape: being truly alone with God and without an agenda. It is a rare and often unsettling feeling to stop doing and just *be*. Yet as strange as it feels to actively seek opportunities to "cease striving" (Psalm 46:10 NASB), the result of doing so consistently can be life changing. We can find clarity in the silence.

Let's define solitude as being completely alone with God, away from all human contact, for an extended period of time. Solitude is stepping out the back door of your noisy life of to-do lists and demanding relationships and breathing in some fresh air. Solitude is being refreshed and restored by the natural rhythms of life that God Himself established. And solitude is taking time to listen for the "still small voice" (1 Kings 19:12 KJV) by which God speaks to your soul and tells you that you are His beloved. Sometimes, doing nothing is the best thing you can do for your people and for yourself.

Jesus modeled solitude as an integral strategic component of His leadership. Consider the following:

- When preparing for the tests of leadership and public ministry, Jesus spent forty days alone in the desert (Matthew 4:1–11).
- Before Jesus chose His twelve apostles from among His followers, He spent the entire night alone in the desert hills (Luke 6:12–13).
- When Jesus received the news of the death of John the Baptist, He withdrew in a boat to a solitary place (Matthew 14:13).
- After the miraculous feeding of the five thousand, Jesus went up in the hills by Himself (Matthew 14:23).

When He was preparing to lead, needing to make important decisions, grieving, and dealing with praise and recognition, Jesus modeled for us the value of spending time alone to stay on track with God.

Spending daily time with God in solitude enables you to make the difficult choices of leadership. Jesus used the solitude of the early morning hours so that He could receive the Father's guidance for His ministry to determine the best use of His time. In Mark 1:32–38, we read:

That evening after sunset the people brought to Jesus all the sick and demon-possessed. The whole town gathered at the door, and Jesus healed many who had various diseases. He also drove out many demons, but he would not let the demons speak because they knew who he was.

Very early in the morning, while it was still dark, Jesus got up, left the house and went off to a solitary place, where he prayed. Simon and his companions went to look for him, and when they found him, they exclaimed: "Everyone is looking for you!"

Jesus replied, "Let us go somewhere else—to the nearby villages—so I can preach there also. That is why I have come."

Did you notice these words? "Very early in the morning, while it was still dark, Jesus got up, left the house and went off to a solitary place, where he prayed." This action strengthened Jesus' resolve to spend His precious time doing the primary work for which He had come—preaching the forgiveness of sins and reconciliation with God—rather than doing the good and popular things of healing and driving out demons. Imagine Jesus' intense compassion for the sick and the demon-possessed people He would have to leave. Imagine the strong temptation to stay and use His healing powers to the delight of all and to bring comfort to His heart, so burdened as it was for lost and suffering humanity.

We believe that Jesus was able to resist doing merely good work and stay focused on His God-given mission because of the time He spent alone with His heavenly Father. In solitude and prayer, away from the hopes and hurts of those who looked to Him with high expectations, Jesus received guidance and strength from God.

PAUSE AND REFLECT

When was the last time you intentionally spent a significant amount of time with God in solitude—and that means without a to-do list or prayer list? When was the last time you sat quietly in God's presence and listened for His "still small voice"? If you can't remember, consider that a clue as to why your life and leadership may seem stuck and unsatisfying. If you can remember and it was more than a week ago, you need to spend time alone with God in the immediate future.

In fact, take a few minutes to be alone with God right now. Put your hands on your knees, palms down. Think of the concerns you have at this moment. When a concern comes to mind, imagine laying it at the foot of the cross. When no more concerns come to mind, turn your hands palms up in a posture of receiving what God wants to give you. Contemplate some aspect of His character, such as His mercy, His love, His grace, or His power. Listen for His voice. Recite Psalm 46:10 in this way:

> Be still, and know that I am God.
> Be still, and know.
> Be still.
> Be.

14

THE HABIT OF PRACTICING PRAYER

One day Jesus was praying in a certain place. When he finished, one of his disciples said to him, "Lord, teach us to pray, just as John taught his disciples."

Luke 11:1

Solitude may be the most elusive of the five Being Habits for us to develop, but prayer is the habit that requires the most unlearning and revising of old patterns and ways. So maybe it is no real surprise that, of all the things the disciples could have asked Jesus to teach them, their only request recorded in Scripture is "Teach us to pray" (Luke 11:1). The disciples saw the power that came when Jesus prayed, and they longed for their prayers to yield the same kind of results. But—as the disciples needed to learn—prayer is not a technique; it is simply a conversation with God.

Prayer is also an essential act of the will that demonstrates whether we are really serious about living and leading like Jesus. Without prayer, we will never be able to either connect our plans and leadership efforts to God's plan for His kingdom or engage the spiritual resources that Jesus promised when He sent His Holy Spirit. Seeking God's will through prayer, waiting in faith for an answer, obeying His instruction when it comes, and being at peace with the outcome will make your leadership a lot like Jesus'.

The power of prayer in one's life truly is immeasurable. Oswald Chambers wrote, "If you will swing the door of your life fully open and pray to your Father who is in the secret place, every public thing in your life will be marked with the lasting imprint of the presence of God."[1] We will see the public results of a life spent in prayer as we consider the example Jesus gave us to follow.

JESUS' PRAYER IN GETHSEMANE

Nowhere in the Bible is found a more powerful model of praying like Jesus than in the dark hours in Gethsemane the night He was betrayed. This was a time of almost unbearable pressure and stress:

> Jesus went with his disciples to a place called Gethsemane, and he said to them, "Sit here while I go over there and pray." He took Peter and the two sons of Zebedee along with him, and he began to be sorrowful and troubled. Then he said to them, "My soul is overwhelmed with sorrow to the point of death. Stay here and keep watch with me."
>
> Going a little farther, he fell with his face to the ground and prayed, "My Father, if it is possible, may this cup be taken from me. Yet not as I will, but as you will." (Matthew 26:36–39)

Jesus' prayer in the Garden of Gethsemane is an excellent example for leaders. Let's look at four instructive aspects.

1. *Where did Jesus pray and why?* He went off by Himself for prayer. Alone with God, Jesus could freely pour out His heart to the Father, knowing the Father understands the broken language of sighs and groans.

2. *What was Jesus' posture in prayer?* Jesus fell on His face before His Father, indicating His agony, extreme sorrow, and humility. At other times Jesus prayed kneeling or looking up to heaven with His eyes open. The posture of the heart is more important than the posture of the body, but prostrating our physical selves before God helps our heart posture.

3. *What did Jesus ask in prayer?* Jesus asked, "If it is possible, may this cup be taken from me" (v. 39). He was asking if He could avoid the suffering of the cross. But notice the way Jesus couched His request: "If it is possible." He left the decision to the Father when He said, "Yet not as I will, but as you will" (v. 39). Although Jesus was keenly aware of the bitter suffering He was to undergo, He freely subjugated His desire to the Father. He based His own willingness upon the Father's will.

4. *What was the answer to Jesus' prayer?* God's answer was that His will—the will of the Father—would be done. The cup of suffering on the cross did not pass from Jesus, for He had presented that petition with the willingness to defer to His Father's will. God answered Jesus' prayer and then fortified Him for the mission He had come to fulfill: "An angel from heaven appeared to him and strengthened him" (Luke 22:43).

As a leader, doing the right thing for the right reasons might require you to drink a bitter cup of ridicule, rejection, or anger. Your human tendency will be to try to avoid that pain. Leading like Jesus will call you to lean in closer to hear from Him how you are to proceed in faith. He will fortify you, enabling you to trust Him to provide you with the courage you need to do the right thing and finish the task.

THE POWER OF PREEMPTIVE PRAYER

When we want to lead like Jesus, prayer becomes our first response, not our last resort. Preemptive prayer is our most powerful, most immediately accessible, most useful resource for responding to the moment-to-moment challenges of life.

Phil's poem shows the possibilities of prayer.

Just Suppose

Just suppose, when I pray, there really is someone listening who
    cares about me and wants to know what is on my mind.
Just suppose, when I pray, it changes me and my view of how
    the universe operates and who is involved.
Just suppose I put my doubts aside for a minute and consider
    the possibility that someone who knew me before I was born
    loves me, warts and all, without condition or reservation, no
    matter how badly I have behaved in the past.
Just suppose a prayer was my first response instead of my last
    resort when facing a new challenge or an old temptation.
Just suppose I lived each day knowing that there is an
    inexhaustible supply of love for me to pass along to others.
Just suppose.

We believe all of these *just suppose* things are true. *Just suppose* they are true for you too.

THE ACTS METHOD OF PRAYER

People often ask us how to pray. Again, prayer is not a technique; it is essentially a conversation with God. We all need to develop our own style of conversing with the Father. For those of you who would like a framework to get started, we suggest the ACTS approach. The simple acronym ACTS can help you remember four basic parts of prayer: Adoration, Confession, Thanksgiving, and Supplication. In addition to helping many beginners in prayer, this method has also served as a compass for weather-beaten veterans. Try it for a few days.

Adoration. All prayer should begin with adoration. Tell the Lord that you love Him and appreciate Him for who He is: "Yours, LORD, is the greatness and the power and the glory and the majesty and the splendor, for everything in heaven and earth is yours. Yours, LORD, is the kingdom; you are exalted as head over all" (1 Chronicles 29:11).

Confession. When we come into the presence of a holy God, we recognize our sins: we all fall short of God's glory. Therefore, our first response to adoring God is confession: "If we confess our sins, he is faithful and just and will forgive us our sins and purify us from all unrighteousness" (1 John 1:9).

Thanksgiving. Thanksgiving is our heartfelt expression of gratitude to God for all He has done in creation and in redemption. Thank God specifically for all that He has done for you. As the old hymn says, "Count your blessings, name them one by one. Count your many blessings; see what God has done."[2] What if tomorrow you only had the things that you thanked God for today? Toothpaste, air, water, clothes, family, job—you name it. Take note of the scripture: "Sing and make music from your heart to the Lord, always giving thanks to God the Father for everything, in the name of our Lord Jesus Christ" (Ephesians 5:19–20).

Supplication. Finally, we get to the part of prayer where most of us start and too often never get past. Supplication is asking for what we need. Start by praying about other people's needs and then ask God to meet your own needs. It's okay to have a big wish list. According to God's Word, we can ask with confidence: "Ask and it will be given to you; seek and you will find; knock and the door will be opened to you" (Matthew 7:7).

PAUSE AND REFLECT

One of the most revealing questions we can ask a leadership candidate is, "How is your prayer life?" The answer will speak volumes about where and how the leader might lead.

Here's a question for you: How is *your* prayer life?

15

THE HABIT OF KNOWING AND APPLYING SCRIPTURE

All Scripture is God-breathed and is useful for teaching, rebuking, correcting and training in righteousness, so that the servant of God may be thoroughly equipped for every good work.

2 Timothy 3:16–17

It is through Scripture that you come to know God and His ways. In the pages of His Word, God invites you to know Him and experience His love. In Scripture you discover that God loves you, He has great plans for you, and He created you perfectly to accomplish a specific purpose. The study of Scripture equips us to fulfill God's plan for us. Scripture also instructs us how to treat one another, how to love as we have been loved, and, yes, how to lead like Jesus.

Consider now these five practical ways you can cultivate the habit of knowing and applying Scripture: hearing, reading, studying, memorizing, and meditating. We pray that today you will begin the adventure of knowing God through Scripture.

HEAR THE WORD

One way to receive the Word is to hear it from someone else. Even a child or a person who cannot read can hear the Bible. Jesus said, "If anyone has ears to hear, let him hear" (Mark 4:23). Hearing with our ears leads to hearing with our hearts. Later, Paul wrote this: "Faith comes from hearing the message, and the message is heard through the word about Christ" (Romans 10:17). Among the many opportunities to hear God's Word today are audiobooks and a variety of social media.

The parable of the sower, found in Matthew 13:3–23, lists four kinds of hearers of the Word. The apathetic hearer hears the Word but does not understand it (v. 19); the superficial hearer receives the Word temporarily but does not let it take root in the heart (vv. 20–21); and the preoccupied hearer receives the Word but lets the worries of this world and the desire for other things choke it out (v. 22). The reproducing hearer, though, receives the Word, understands it, and bears fruit (v. 23). Which kind of hearer are you?

PAUSE AND REFLECT

One way to apply what you hear is to ask yourself the following questions after you hear each Scripture passage and jot down your thoughts.

- What did God say to me?
- How does my life measure up to God's standards and instructions?

- What actions will I take to align my life with His message?
- What truth in the passage do I need to study further?
- What truth can I share with another person today?

READ THE WORD

The second way you learn God's Word is to read it: "Blessed is the one who reads aloud the words of this prophecy, and blessed are those who hear it and take to heart what is written in it, because the time is near" (Revelation 1:3). Be sure to allow time for reflection after you read.

Choose a short passage of Scripture. If you read too much at once, you may find it challenging to reflect on its meaning or allow God to speak directly to you and your situation. Start with a passage of manageable length, like these verses from Psalm 103: "Praise the LORD, my soul; all my inmost being, praise his holy name. Praise the LORD, my soul, and forget not all his benefits" (vv. 1–2).

Balance your reading of the Word. Be sure that your reading of God's Word includes both the Old Testament and the New Testament. God will speak to you through every word in His Word. Jesus said, "'Everything must be fulfilled that is written about me in the Law of Moses, the Prophets and the Psalms.' Then he opened [the disciples'] minds so they could understand the Scriptures" (Luke 24:44–45). The Bible contains many passages that point to Jesus. You will want to read about Him in the sections mentioned in Luke as well as throughout the Bible. Apply the Word to your life each day. Ask God to show you what His Word means to you and for your life. Jesus instructed, "If you love me, keep my commands" (John 14:15).

Every time you apply the Word of God to your life, you grow closer to Him. Every time you fail to apply it, you leave the Word, like scattered seed, beside the road, where Satan can steal it. When you read God's Word, respond to it with prayer and obedience. Scripture teaches us that obedience is always about our love for our heavenly Father.

STUDY THE WORD

Studying the Word means learning more about its meaning and application. Knowing God's Word more deeply will enable us to follow this New Testament example: "Now the Berean Jews were of more noble character than those in Thessalonica, for they received the message with great eagerness and examined the Scriptures every day to see if what Paul said was true" (Acts 17:11).

With study, you begin to handle God's Word more effectively. Bible study is an in-depth look into the Scriptures: the goal is to learn more than you would during a simple overview or in a devotional reading. Study involves, for instance, comparing one Bible passage to another or searching through the Scriptures for the answer to a question. Bible study often includes gaining additional information through commentaries and study helps.

MEMORIZE THE WORD

When you commit God's Word to memory, it lives in you, you live in it, and God's promises become your possessions. The psalmist recognized this truth: "How can a young person stay on the path of purity? By living according to your word. . . . I have hidden your word in my heart that I might not sin against you" (Psalm 119:9, 11).

In the account of Jesus' temptation in the wilderness (Matthew 4:1–11), Jesus set the example for us. He used Scripture as the sword of the Spirit against Satan, even when Satan misused Scripture to fuel the temptation. In addition to helping you gain victory over sin, memorized Scripture helps you answer people who have questions about your faith. Being able to recite Scripture verses by heart also helps you to reflect on them and gives you direction for your daily life at any moment. Finally, memorizing scriptures enables us to obey this God-given command: "Always be prepared to give an answer to everyone who asks you to give the reason for the hope that you have" (1 Peter 3:15).

When Phyllis was eight years old, a group came to her school and offered students a chance to go to a two-week summer camp—with swimming, tennis, campfires, and s'mores—and it wouldn't cost them a cent. The only cost was memorizing three hundred Scripture verses.

Phyllis was up to the challenge. Her parents agreed it was a good commitment to make and offered to help. So Phyllis got up at 6:00 a.m. each day, memorized a passage, and recited it to her father, who was pastor of a church. Every morning he would pray, *Lord, help Phyllis remember these scriptures. Plant them as seeds in her heart.* At the end of each week, Phyllis would recite all the week's verses for her father, who would sign a form to verify that she had memorized them.

By the end of the school year, Phyllis had memorized all three hundred verses and earned two weeks at camp. But she had not considered two key things: First, she had never been away from home. And second, no one else at her school had memorized the verses, so she wouldn't know anyone at camp.

On Wednesday of the first week, Phyllis called home in tears and begged her mother to come get her. Her mother persuaded her to stay until Saturday. When Phyllis got home, she was disappointed that she had worked so hard and not enjoyed the reward.

Phyllis didn't yet know that her real reward was learning—among many other things—that she never had to be afraid. In Isaiah 43:1 she had learned that God knew her by name, and she was His. She had learned in Jeremiah 33:3 that God would answer her and tell her "great and unsearchable things." In Ephesians 3:20 she had learned that God would do "immeasurably more" than anything she could "ask or imagine"—and she had a big imagination.

Eight-year-old Phyllis had no idea how God would use those seeds she had worked so hard to plant in her heart. Many years later, though, when her husband of twenty-two years collapsed in front of her, Phyllis had in her mind the words of Jeremiah 29:11, a verse she had memorized as a child: "I know the plans I have for you . . . plans to prosper you and not to harm you, plans to give you hope and a future."

Sitting with her daughter in a waiting room, Phyllis looked up as the doctor came to the doorway and said, "I am sorry. Sometimes the first sign of heart disease is fatal."

Immediately Phyllis heard, "I know the plans I have for you . . . plans to prosper you and not to harm you, plans to give you hope and a future." *This doesn't feel like hope and a future*, she thought. Then, almost like a movie playing in her mind, Proverbs 3:5–6 appeared: "Trust in the LORD with all your heart and lean not on your own understanding; in all your ways submit to him, and he will make your paths straight." She said out loud, "It is about trusting You."

Phyllis never could have imagined that a little more than three years later, she would marry again. Throughout the next nineteen years, she depended on Scripture to teach her about loving unconditionally, blending a family, and serving them. Then the news came that her second husband had lung cancer. How could that be? He was not a smoker, and he looked healthy. Phyllis leaned on God for the next several months as her big, strong husband went from walking alone to walking with a cane, using a walker, needing a wheelchair, and then resting in a hospice bed. Every day she reminded herself of what she knew about God from Scripture: *He loves me; He has great plans for me; He will never leave me.* When her husband was released to his new life, Phyllis knew she could still trust God with all her heart. It is amazing that, beginning when she was eight years old, God used His Word to prepare Phyllis for every part of her journey. Her father's prayer was answered: those verses planted in her heart were seeds of truth that took deep root in her life.

PAUSE AND REFLECT

1. Choose a few verses that have touched you.
2. Write each verse on a note card and place it in a prominent place so that you can review it while you do other tasks.
3. Turn it over in your mind; savor every word.
4. Review it often for as long as it takes you to store the message in your mind. Then move to another verse.

MEDITATE ON GOD'S WORD

Another way you live in the Word and the Word lives in you is to think about it or meditate on its truth. As the psalmist said, "Blessed is the one . . . whose delight is in the law of the LORD, and who meditates on his law day and night" (Psalm 1:1–2).

You meditate on God's Word when you focus on a specific verse of Scripture in order to more fully understand all that it says. Select a key verse in a passage you have just read. Ask the Holy Spirit for His revelation as you meditate.

Here are some practical ways to meditate on God's Word:

1. Read the verses before and after your selected verse to establish the theme and setting. That information will aid you in interpretation. Write a summary of the passage.

2. Write the verse(s) in your own words. Read your paraphrase aloud.

3. Now read the verse over and over again, emphasizing a different word each time. For example, in the verse "I can do all things through Christ who strengthens me" (Philippians 4:13 NKJV), first emphasize the word *I*, then the word *can*, and so on. This exercise helps each word yield its full impact.

4. State the opposite meaning of the verse. For instance: "I can't do anything if Christ does not strengthen me." What impact does the verse have on you now?

5. Write at least two important words from the verse. To relate the Scripture to your current life situation, ask a few of these questions about the two words: What? Why? Where? Who? How? For example: "What can I do?" All things. "Why?" Because Christ strengthens me. "Who strengthens me?" Christ.

6. Personalize the verse. Ask the Holy Spirit to use its truth to speak to a need, a challenge, an opportunity, or a failure in your life. Then determine what you will do in response to this verse as it relates to your life. Be specific.

7. Repeat the verse back to God in your prayer time with Him. Put your own name or situation in the verse.

8. Refer to other passages that emphasize the truth of the

verse. List any thoughts you might not understand or ideas you might have difficulty applying in your life. Seek out instruction or help in these areas.

9. Write out a way you can use the verse to help another person—and then do so.

PAUSE AND REFLECT

Are you actively seeking God's guidance by spending time reading the Bible? What is He currently saying to you?

16

THE HABIT OF MAINTAINING
SUPPORTIVE RELATIONSHIPS

Though one may be overpowered, two can defend
themselves. A cord of three strands is not quickly broken.

Ecclesiastes 4:12

Among the twelve men He called out to be His apostles, Jesus had
a small group of three—Peter, James, and John—with whom He
seemed to have a particularly close relationship. He took these three
with Him to the Mount of Transfiguration, where He revealed to
them, in confidence, the true nature of His being (Matthew 17:1–9).
These same three men were present when Jesus raised from the dead
the daughter of a synagogue leader (Mark 5:21–43). And the most
poignant episode involving this circle of friends occurred on the night
Jesus was arrested and began His final journey to the cross: Jesus
asked them to follow deeper into the garden with Him (Matthew
26:37–38). But Peter, James, and John—invited along to support their
Friend in His agonizing anticipation of the cross—fell asleep.

As this last scene so powerfully illustrates, leadership can
be a lonely business filled with great amounts of soul-draining
human interaction but little soul-filling intimacy. Leaders need

safe-harbor relationships in which they can lay down all the armor and weapons they need to face the world and can relax in confidential and unguarded conversation. Without these safe relationships, leaders become vulnerable to two debilitating frames of mind and spirit: the victim and the martyr. Allowed to blossom into either resentment or a justification for seeking EGO-soothing instant gratification, these twin demons have been the downfall of many a leader in every walk of life.

Jesus emphasized the importance of communion of spirit when He prayed for His followers to attain the joy that He Himself had in His unity and fellowship with His Father. In John 15:9, 12–15 Jesus told His disciples:

> "As the Father has loved me, so have I loved you. Now remain in my love.... My command is this: Love each other as I have loved you. Greater love has no one than this: to lay down one's life for one's friends. You are my friends if you do what I command. I no longer call you servants, because a servant does not know his master's business. Instead, I have called you friends, for everything that I learned from my Father I have made known to you."

When we rely on our own perspectives of how we are doing, we are bound to slip into convenient rationalizations or unknowingly encounter blind spots, both of which can quickly undermine our integrity as well as the trust of those we lead.

TRUTH TELLERS

We all need trusted truth tellers—preferably people not directly affected by our leadership—who can help us keep on course. If you can't name any active truth tellers in your life, or if you have avoided or undervalued the ones you have, it's time to make a change. Truth tellers are probably your greatest resource for growth. Ken's father used to tell him, "I learned in the navy that if you don't hear from your people about any problems, watch out, because you are about to go over the side. You have mutiny on your hands, because the people around you don't feel valued—and therefore they have cut you off from the truth."

Too often a self-serving leader will silence valuable feedback by killing the messenger. Eventually the leader is fired. Although people were available who could have given the leader helpful information, the leader cut off the workers' opportunity to grow and to communicate ideas that would have improved the leader's own skills.

Feedback is a gift. If somebody gives you a gift, what do you say? "Thank you!" Then ask more questions in order to understand what is being said and why: "What made you think that?" "How long has this been an issue?" "Don't name names, but can you tell me more about how your coworkers are feeling?" "Whom do you suggest I talk to about this situation?" And maybe even "Why hasn't anyone approached me before now?"

Truth tellers are willing to be honest if they know you are going to listen. Your listening doesn't mean you have to do everything they say, but they want to know you have heard them. If you let yourself be a bit vulnerable in the process, the give-and-take can be rich and valuable.

> Two are better than one, because they have a good return for
> their labor: If either of them falls down, one can help the other
> up. But pity anyone who falls and has no one to help them up.
> (Ecclesiastes 4:9–10)

We encourage you to contact people you know and form an accountability relationship or group that meets for regular times of truth telling.

Being open to feedback from other people is not the only way to grow; being willing to disclose our own vulnerabilities, flaws, and sins to other people is another. All of us fall short of being who God wants us to be; we fall short of being who *we* want to be! So don't be afraid to share specific points of vulnerability. Being open is one of the most powerful ways to build relationships with the people you're leading. They know you're not perfect, so don't act as if you are. More times than not, they know your imperfections long before you reveal them. Colleen Barrett, president emerita of Southwest Airlines, puts it this way: "People admire your skills, but they love your vulnerability."[1]

However, disclosing your vulnerabilities doesn't mean divulging all your inner thoughts. Rather, you want to share only task-relevant information or struggles you are working on as a leader. If a truth teller says you're not a good listener, it's wonderful to go in front of the team and say something like this: "Bill was kind enough to share feedback with me about my listening. I didn't realize that when you say things to me, I jump right into my own agenda. But now I know—and I would like to improve. The only way I can listen better is if you help me." As Proverbs 27:6 says: "Wounds from a friend can be trusted, but an enemy multiplies kisses."

SMALL-GROUP FELLOWSHIP

In *Leadership by the Book*—which Ken and Phil wrote with Bill Hybels—one of the central characters explains how he got into trouble after a successful start at becoming a leader: "When I boil it down, it was a combination of ego and self-imposed isolation."[2]

As we commit to becoming more like Jesus in the way we lead, it is vital to note how He combated the loneliness and isolation that often come with leadership. Throughout His earthly ministry, Jesus had all kinds of relationships with all kinds of people. Hundreds, even thousands, of people flocked to Him everywhere He went. Yet He chose twelve men as disciples to entrust with His mission and, from those, three inner-circle confidants—Peter, James, and John—to lean on in crucial times.

If you are to grow in your daily walk as a Jesus-like leader, you need similar supportive relationships. The temptations and challenges to be an EGO-driven, fear-motivated leader are going to continue and will probably intensify. The value of having safe-harbor relationships of support and accountability cannot be overemphasized. As one New Testament writer put it, "Let us consider how we may spur one another on toward love and good deeds, not giving up meeting together . . . but encouraging one another" (Hebrews 10:24–25).

PAUSE AND REFLECT

Name the special people in your life who love you enough to tell you what you need to hear. What are you doing to nurture and strengthen those special relationships?

Who in your life needs you to hold them accountable? Do you love them enough to tell them what they need to know?

Listed below are sample questions for inner-circle accountability conversations:

- Where do you see or sense God at work in your life right now?
- What truth, command, or redirection has God been making clear to you lately?
- What is something you need to start doing? What's holding you back?
- What is something you need to stop doing? What's keeping you from stopping?
- What gaps—if any—exist between your saying and your doing?

WHAT DECISION WILL YOU MAKE?

The world needs to see God, and the only way some people will see Him is if they see God through us. That's why each of us has a decision to make: Will we choose to lead like everyone else, or will we choose to lead like Jesus by practicing the five Being Habits?

When former professional football player Rosey Grier spoke at a Lead Like Jesus event, he shared a compelling personal example of the importance of being prepared to lead like Jesus:

You know what I wanted to do as a football player? I wanted to carry the ball. But the Giants wouldn't let me because I was too big. I played in five world championship games with the Giants and then got traded to the LA Rams. They wouldn't let me carry the football either—they put me on defense.

One day we're playing the Green Bay Packers. They drove from their five-yard line down to our five-yard line, so we called a time-out. Our guys huddled up and said, "They're going to score on us. Let's run a blitz."

Now, they didn't know we were going to run a blitz. So the quarterback struts out and says, "Everybody go down!" Then Deacon Jones, Merlin Olsen, Lamar Lundy, and I start coming after him. While he was fading back with the ball, he closed his eyes. Deacon, Merlin, and Lamar jumped on him, and there was no place left for me to jump on him.

Then the football popped up, just like that. I'm looking up at that football. All my life I've been wanting to carry that football. I heard a voice in my head say, "You're supposed to yell out, 'Ball!'" But the week before, I had yelled out, "Ball!" and Merlin got the football and started running down the sideline. I was so mad! I caught up to him and said, "Say, Merlin, let me carry the football some." He said, "No, man, I'm carrying it all the way!" So I didn't block for him—and he didn't make it either.

So I'm looking at that football, and I have to make a decision. I don't want to say, "Ball!" because I want to run ninety-five yards for a touchdown myself. But as I'm standing there, with my hands up in the air, that old voice in my head says, "Can you *catch*?"

You know what? I had never practiced catching. When I had an opportunity to run ninety-five yards for a touchdown, I wasn't able to do it because I was not prepared.

Today is the day to make your decision if you haven't already. Will you decide to lead like Jesus? If so, will you choose to get prepared to run the leadership race by putting into practice the five Being Habits that Jesus modeled?

PAUSE AND REFLECT

How ready are you to lead like Jesus today? Answering the following questions about the Being Habits will give you an idea.

- Accepting and Abiding in God's Unconditional Love—Do you sense God's unconditional love for you today? If not, why do you think that's the case?
- Solitude—Are you ready to be alone with Jesus on a regular basis? If so, what's your plan for being consistent? If not, why do you think you're hesitant?
- Prayer—What will you do to strengthen your prayer life and communicate with Jesus on a regular basis?
- Bible Study—Are you actively seeking the Lord's guidance by spending time studying His Holy Word? If not, why not?
- Supportive Relationships—Do you have a small group of like-minded friends with whom you can be open and vulnerable? If not, where might you look? If so, what do you do to nurture and strengthen those relationships?

PART IV

THE HEAD OF A GREAT LEADER

> Do not conform to the pattern of this world, but be transformed by the renewing of your mind. Then you will be able to test and approve what God's will is—his good, pleasing and perfect will.
>
> Romans 12:2

The journey of becoming a great leader starts in the *heart* with motivation and intent. If you don't get the heart right, your leadership will never reflect how Jesus led. Then, when we realize that God is our primary authority and audience and that we are here to please Him alone, our good intentions travel to our *heads*. That is where we store our perspectives on life and leadership: specifically, all great leaders know not only *whose* they are, but also *who* they are. They are aware that the purpose of their lives is already embedded within them, put there by God. As Ephesians 2:10 says, "We are God's handiwork, created in Christ Jesus to do good works, which God prepared in advance for us to do."

So we will start this section on the head of a great leader by helping you develop a compelling vision for your life that will tell you and those you influence who you are (your purpose), where you are going (your picture of the future), and what will guide your journey (your values).[1]

Once we have focused on you and how the vision for your life will have an impact on others, we will turn our attention to the need for developing a compelling vision for your team or organization. Of course, throughout our discussion we will be focusing on Jesus' intentions for Himself and for us.

DEVELOPING YOUR OWN COMPELLING VISION

When I preach the gospel, I cannot boast, since I am compelled to preach.

1 Corinthians 9:16

The goal of this chapter is to help you develop a compelling vision for your life. This vision will be important in guiding and aligning the efforts of those who are to follow you so that their relationship with you is not built on a false foundation of who you are.

Our experience tells us that few people have a clear, compelling vision for themselves, even though God has one for each of us. And how do you make a decision about what you are going to do with your time if you don't have a compelling vision that tells you your purpose, reflects your picture of the future, and reminds you of your values?

YOUR LIFE PURPOSE

We all share a common purpose: "Whatever you do, do it all for the glory of God" (1 Corinthians 10:31). But each of us also has a specific purpose, a personalized reason for being. Note that a purpose is different from a goal, in that it does not have a beginning or an end; your purpose is the meaning of the journey of your life, not the destination. Your purpose is your calling, the reason you were created, the place where your passion and giftedness meet. In the context of leadership, your purpose must include serving the best interests of those you lead, or your "leadership" becomes manipulation and exploitation, the absolute opposite of leading like Jesus.

The following is a simple process that will help you create a good first draft of your life purpose.[1] First, list some personal characteristics you feel good about. These are God-given traits that are unique to you.

Use nouns like these:

patience	sales ability	energy
enthusiasm	intellect	artistic ability
physical	charm	role model
strength	problem-	creativity
wit	solving ability	teaching ability
sense of humor	diplomacy	

For example, Ken chose *sense of humor, people skills, teaching skills,* and *role model.*

_____

_____

_____

_____

Next, list ways you successfully interact with people. These have to do with your unique, God-given personality. Use verbs like these:

teach	encourage	love
inspire	plan	coach
produce	stimulate	help
manage	act	write
educate	lead	
motivate	sell	

Ken picked *educate, help, inspire,* and *motivate.*

_____

_____

_____

Finally, visualize what your perfect world would be—one that would make Jesus smile. What would people do or say? Write a description of this perfect world.

To Ken, a perfect world is *where everyone is aware of the presence of God in their lives and realizes they are here to serve, not to be served.*

_____

_____

_____

Now, combine two of your nouns, two of your verbs, and your definition of your perfect world, and you'll have a good start on a definition of your life purpose.

Ken's life purpose is to be *a loving teacher and role model of simple truths who helps and motivates myself and others to be aware of the presence of God in our lives and realize we are here to serve, not to be served.*

_____

_____

_____

_____

Remember, this is your first draft. Share it with important people in your life and see how they respond. Feel free to make changes; determining your life purpose is an ongoing process.

YOUR PICTURE OF THE FUTURE

Your picture of the future is all about where you are heading in your life and, in many ways, how you'd like to be remembered. In fact, the essence of your picture of the future might be the epitaph on your tombstone. While it might sound morbid, it is actually helpful to think of your own obituary as your picture of the future.

We first got this idea when we read about Alfred Nobel's experience in the late nineteenth century. Alfred Nobel was the inventor of dynamite. When his brother Ludvig died in France, a newspaper mistakenly printed an obituary about Alfred instead of Ludvig. As a result, Alfred had the unusual experience of reading his own obituary. To his dismay, the focal point of the piece was the destruction brought about through his invention of dynamite. Devastated to think he would be remembered that way, Alfred gathered friends and loved ones around him and asked them, "What's the opposite of destruction?" The almost unanimous reply was "Peace." As a result, Alfred redesigned his life and set aside the bulk of his estate to establish the Nobel Prize so that he would be remembered for peace, not destruction.

To determine your picture of the future, we want you to write your own obituary. This is not something you can put together as quickly as you did the first draft of your life purpose. We suggest you spend some time on it and then share it with some of your loved ones—not to scare them but to get their feedback. Ask them, "Is this the way you would like to remember me?"

To give you an example, the following is an obituary Ken wrote about himself. When he shared it with his wife, Margie, at first she thought he was getting a little dark, but then she got into it and helped him write it.

Ken Blanchard was a loving teacher and living example of simple truths whose books and speeches on leadership, management, and life helped motivate himself and others to awaken to the presence of God in their lives and to realize they are here to serve, not to be served. He continually inspired, challenged, and equipped people to live, love, and lead like Jesus. He was a loving child of God, son, brother, spouse, father, grandfather, uncle, cousin, friend, and colleague who strove to find a balance between success, significance, and surrender. He had a spiritual peace about him that permitted him to say no in a loving manner to people and to projects that got him off purpose. He knew full well that BUSY stands for Being Under Satan's Yoke. He was a person of high energy who was able to see the positive in any event. No matter what happened, he could find a lesson or message in it. Ken Blanchard trusted God's unconditional love and believed *he was God's beloved*. Ken valued integrity, walked his talk, and was a 185-pound lean and mean golfing machine. He will be missed, because wherever he went, he made the world a better place.

Ken recognizes that some of the things mentioned in the obituary are goals or hoped-for outcomes, such as being able to say no in a loving manner to both people and projects that get him off purpose: Ken admits he still has never heard a bad idea. As for being a 185-pound lean and mean golfing machine, that is also an ongoing aspiration.

So have fun writing your obituary. Share your truth about yourself as well as some hoped-for results of your life.

YOUR CORE VALUES

It has been said that the most important thing in life is to decide what's most important. Your values are the beliefs you find most important: you feel strongly about them and choose them over other alternatives.

When you were a kid, your parents and other adults tended to define your values, but at some point in life we all choose what is most important to us. Your leader at work might value results more than people, and you might be the opposite. People don't all value the same things. Some people value wealth and power, and others are more concerned with safety or survival. Success is a value; integrity and relationships are values as well. The following is a sample list of some personal values. If the list doesn't include things you value, write them in the blank spaces.

truth	originality	security
wisdom	service	resources
power	respect	love
commitment	freedom	excellence
courage	order	fun
recognition	integrity	responsiveness
excitement	spirituality	relationships
learning	peace	success
creativity	cooperation	_____
honesty	loyalty	_____
happiness	humor	_____

When you turn your life over to the Lord, He will give you a different perspective on what you value. Given that fact, circle the *ten* values from this list that are most meaningful to you. If you have trouble narrowing down your top values, combine a couple. For example, Ken combined two words and included *spiritual peace* as an important value for him.

As you try to determine what your values are, we want you to start with a long list of ten. But fewer than ten is better, particularly if you want your values to guide your behavior. Some maintain that more than five values is too many and can be immobilizing.[2]

Now look at those ten circled values and underline the *five* values that are more meaningful to your life than the rest. Take your time. Making these choices can be difficult.

Now here's the part that may take you even longer. Study those five remaining values and *rank them* from most important (#1) to least important (#5).

Your number one value is your core value, something you want to be true about you no matter what you're doing. If, for example, your number one value is integrity, living without integrity is not an option.

Why did we want you to rank your values? Because values exist in dynamic tension with one another. For example, if you value financial growth but integrity is your core value, you will look at any activities that could lead to financial gain through the lens of integrity, because you value integrity more than profit.

Ken ordered his values like this: *spiritual peace, integrity, love,* and *joy.*

How do you know if you're living according to a particular value? First, you have to define that value as specifically as possible. If you don't define each value, it will have little meaning to you or to anyone else. A value like *justice,* for example, can be defined differently by different people. For one, it might mean "equal opportunity." For another, it might mean "fair process." For the third, it might mean "getting my due share."

So take some quiet time to define each of your values, and for each one decide how you would finish this statement:

"I value _____, and I know I am living by this value anytime I . . ."

One of Ken's values is joy, a concept some might think is difficult to define. Ken has written the following:

I value joy, and I know I am living by this value anytime I . . .

- let my playful child express himself;
- wake up feeling grateful for my blessings, for the beauty around me, and for the people in my life;
- smile and am happy and laugh and kid; and
- get into the act of forgetfulness about myself.

Once you have a good grasp of your purpose, your picture of the future, and your values, write them down in a place where you can read them every morning. Doing so will help to set your vision for the day. At night, review the list to see how well you did.

We understand that you might feel intimidated by people who write in their journals in four different colors and include poetry. But at the end of the day, after reviewing your compelling vision, make a simple journal entry. Write affirmations of what you did well that day. Then write *redirections* regarding what you wish you could do over. (That could mean making an apology or two the next day.) In other words, don't create a compelling vision and then never look at it again.

GOALS

You might be wondering where goal setting fits in with developing a personal compelling vision. Goals are not normally considered part of a compelling vision for one's life, but they do help you determine what you want to accomplish on a day-to-day basis.

When it comes to goal setting, you need to remember two things. First, don't establish too many goals. Three to five are the most any individual can focus on at any one time. We believe in the 80/20 rule: 80 percent of what you want to happen in your life comes from about 20 percent of what you focus your attention on. So set goals in the 20 percent that will give you the greatest impact.

Second, make your goals observable and measurable. If you can't measure something, you can't manage it. You need to know what good behavior looks like. The action your goal focuses on needs to be observable. For example, if you are interested in losing weight, you need to know your present weight and your desired weight. Then, on a weekly basis, you can track how well you are doing and either cheer yourself on or redirect your efforts and get back on track.

PAUSE AND REFLECT

In this chapter we gave you a lot of work to do as well as a lot to think about. Study the answers you came up with and review what you have learned about yourself. Remember that assessing your life purpose, your picture of the future, your values, and your goals is an ongoing process.

Finally, consider these two questions: In what specific

way(s) can your recently crafted compelling vision be used for the greater good? And what can you do to glorify God in the context of fulfilling your vision?

JESUS' COMPELLING VISION

"The Son of Man came to seek and to save the lost."

Luke 19:10

A key insight into Jesus' compelling vision for His life is contained in His prayer for His disciples, recorded in John 17. Jesus stayed focused on what He was sent to accomplish in His season of leadership. He told His Father, "I brought glory to you here on earth by completing the work you gave me to do" (John 17:4 NLT). In total obedience and commitment, Jesus stayed on task. He did not seek to take on other projects or the agenda others hoped He would fulfill.

One of the greatest services that leaders can provide followers is constancy of purpose. When the going gets tough, when temptations to short-term success arise, and when distractions or setbacks come, people will look to their leaders to see how they respond. Will they stay on course and remain true to their mission and values, or will they give up and give in to the pressures of the moment?

PAUSE AND REFLECT

List the three things that are most likely to pull you off course as a leader. What impact would changing course or direction have on the morale of the people you lead?

Jesus took responsibility not just for proclaiming God's truth but also for equipping His followers with a full understanding of what they needed to know to carry out their mission: "Now [my disciples] know that everything I have is a gift from you, for I have passed on to them the message you gave me. They accepted it and know that I came from you, and they believe you sent me" (John 17:7–8 NLT). When leaders fail to take the time and effort to ensure that what they have in mind is understood and accepted, they leave themselves open to frustration, an unfulfilled mission, and bewildered and discouraged followers.

It is profoundly significant that the last lesson Jesus taught His disciples on the night of His betrayal was the same one He began with—what it means to be a servant leader. In Luke 22 we read:

[Jesus] took bread, gave thanks and broke it, and gave it to [the disciples in the upper room], saying, "This is my body given for you; do this in remembrance of me."

In the same way, after the supper he took the cup, saying, "This cup is the new covenant in my blood, which is poured out for you." . . .

A dispute also arose among them as to which of them was considered to be greatest. Jesus said to them, "The kings of the Gentiles lord it over them; and those who exercise authority over them call themselves Benefactors. But you are not to be like that. Instead, the greatest among you should be like the youngest, and the one who rules like the one who serves." (vv. 19–20, 24–26)

PAUSE AND REFLECT

Think about the depth of character and the patient love Jesus displayed in that intense moment with His disciples, who within hours would abandon and deny Him. Jesus did not despair over their slowness to grasp what He had repeatedly taught them about leadership. Instead, as the ultimate Servant Leader, Jesus provided what the disciples needed most to develop in their ability to fulfill their mission, and that meant teaching them about servant leadership one more time.

Jesus also felt responsible for the ongoing protection of His followers as, for the last time before His death, He inspired and equipped them for their mission. He told His Father, "While I was with them, I protected them and kept them safe by that name you gave me. None has been lost except the one doomed to destruction so that Scripture would be fulfilled" (John 17:12).

The more difficult and perilous the journey, the more willing leaders must be to maintain constant vigilance regarding the health and safety of their followers. This attentiveness can mean making sure they are properly trained and equipped for their mission. It can mean providing a clear set of operating values and then modeling how to use them as a guide in making decisions when the leader is not there. A leader's vigilance can mean standing up for followers in the face of opposition or unjustified criticism. It can also mean being a good guardian of their trust by telling them the truth and being willing to serve them in areas they are not yet able to tackle on their own. Finally, in Jesus' case, as the Good Shepherd of His followers, Jesus laid down His life so that none might perish (John 10:11, 28).

Looking beyond His time of earthly leadership, Jesus sought to provide for His followers, who would continue to implement the mission He had called them to fulfill. On the last night of His ministry on earth, Jesus prayed:

> "Now I am departing from the world; they are staying in this world, but I am coming to you. Holy Father, you have given me your name; now protect them by the power of your name so that they will be united just as we are. . . . I'm not asking you to take them out of the world, but to keep them safe from the evil one." (John 17:11, 15 NLT)

A truly great and enduring vision will extend beyond an individual's season of leadership. Ideally, a leader seeks to send out the next generation of leaders to meet the challenges of their own season with all the wisdom, knowledge, and spiritual resources the leader can provide them. That is the fruit of great leadership.

Therefore, it is of the greatest significance and encouragement that the prayer Jesus offered on behalf of His first disciples, He offered as well for those who would come after them—including those of us who follow Him today: "My prayer is not for them alone. I pray also for those who will believe in me through their message" (John 17:20).

The "tyranny of the *or*" suggests that you, as a leader, have to choose results *or* people. Yet Jesus modeled a "both/and" approach. In His daily interactions, Jesus elevated the growth and development

of people to the status of an end goal that was every bit as important as other results. Jesus did exactly what His Father called Him
to do, *and* He also focused on the development of the people around
Him. And, true to His compelling vision, Jesus glorified God as He
did both.

In your own season of leadership, you are called to engage in
the same dual purpose. Your family, organization, community,
or office needs to accomplish certain things. That's one purpose.
Following Jesus and leading as He led is another: you are serving
a higher purpose and being held accountable to a higher standard,
and neither may be universally understood or applauded. At the
same time that you attend to the tasks at hand, you will do as Jesus
did and focus on serving people by helping them grow and develop.

CREATING A COMPELLING TEAM/ ORGANIZATIONAL VISION

Jesus came to [the disciples] and said, "All authority in heaven and on earth has been given to me. Therefore go and make disciples of all nations, baptizing them in the name of the Father and of the Son and of the Holy Spirit, and teaching them to obey everything I have commanded you. And surely I am with you always, to the very end of the age."

Matthew 28:18–20

While it's important for you to have a personal compelling vision that tells you who you are (your purpose), where you are going (your picture of the future), and what will guide your journey (your values), it is also important to create such a vision for the teams and organizations you lead.

The focus of leading a team is developing a sense of community and emphasizing that none of us is as smart as all of us. Organizational leadership is more complicated, because you are leading a number of teams or divisions, and the focus is on developing a culture—a pattern of behavior that reflects your approach to your business. Every organization has a culture. If you don't create one that facilitates what you want to accomplish, a culture will develop on its own and could become dysfunctional or work against your purposes.

When we mention that leaders are meant to serve rather than to be served, people often think it means that the leader is trying to please everyone. Yet that is not at all what Jesus means by servant leadership. Did Jesus try to please everyone? When He washed the feet of the disciples and sent them out as His ambassadors, was He commissioning them to do whatever the people wanted them to do? Of course the answer to both those questions is no.

Jesus was completely focused on pleasing His Father, who truly was His Audience of One. And pleasing the Father meant proclaiming the gospel and dying on the cross in order to bring salvation to humankind. Jesus sent His disciples to help people understand the good news and then live according to the values of God's kingdom, not just do whatever they wanted. Jesus made it very clear that what He was asking His followers to do, in His name, would not please everyone. Jesus told the disciples up front that they would be subject to all kinds of resistance and persecution for telling people the truths that they did not want to hear.

THE TWO ROLES OF LEADERSHIP

People skeptical about our approach to great leadership contend that the words *servant* and *leader* don't go together. How can a person both lead *and* serve? People who think that way don't understand the two parts to the great leadership that Jesus exemplified:

1. The visionary role—setting the course and the destination—is the *leadership* aspect.
2. The implementation role—doing things the right way with a focus on serving—is the *servant* aspect.

Some people think leadership is about vision while management is about implementation, but when such a distinction is made, management seems to get a second-class status. We prefer not to distinguish between the two because we consider both to be important leadership roles.

Our point of view is that vision and implementation are two sides of the same coin and are therefore equally important. To maximize results for everyone concerned, you must *lead* by setting the course and direction, and then flip the coin and *serve* by empowering and supporting others in implementation.

THE *LEADERSHIP* ASPECT OF GREAT LEADERSHIP

Effective leadership begins with a clear vision. If your followers don't know where you are going or where you are trying to take them, they will have a hard time getting there. In the classic story *Alice in Wonderland*, Alice learned this lesson when she came to a fork in the road. She asked the Cheshire cat which way she should go. When he asked where she was going, Alice replied that she didn't know. The cat concluded matter-of-factly, "Then it doesn't matter which way you go."[1] Without clear direction, leadership doesn't matter.

A compelling vision provides clear direction and focuses

everyone's energy on getting where they are headed. As we said in the introduction to this section, a compelling vision has three parts:

1. Your purpose. Who are you? What business are you in? What is your family all about?
2. Your picture of the future. Where are you going? What will your future look like if you are living out your purpose?
3. Your values. What will guide your journey? What do you stand for? On what principles will you make decisions?

DEVELOPING A COMPELLING VISION

Your Purpose

What business are you in? What are you trying to accomplish? What is your mission statement? Jesus was clear about what business He and His disciples were in. He called His disciples, not just to become fishermen, but to a greater purpose—to become fishers of men.

An effective mission statement should express a higher purpose for the greater good and give meaning to the efforts of each individual in your organization. When Walt Disney started his theme parks, he knew how to excite people. You could say Disney was, and still is, in the happiness business. Wouldn't you rather be in the happiness business than the theme park business? Being in the happiness business drives everything Disney's cast members (employees) do with and for their guests (customers).

Even if an organization states its mission, if that statement does not support a higher purpose, it will not motivate people. For instance, one congregation said they wanted to be a twenty-four-hour-a-day church. They had a nice facility, and they wanted to keep the rooms busy. But attendance went down because the mission wasn't something the people got excited about. Your purpose needs to inspire people.

At another church, the purpose is more inspiring to the congregation. At the beginning of every service, the minister says, "We believe that a close encounter with Jesus of Nazareth can transform lives. Our mission is to make Jesus smile." Backing up that statement are clear theological values. Attendance has gone up. It's a place where a community comes together with the main purpose of making Jesus smile.

A clear purpose tells you what business you are in. At the Lead Like Jesus ministry, our purpose is "to glorify God by inspiring and equipping people to lead like Jesus." If your organization does not have a clear purpose, if your mission statement is not worded so that everyone understands it, or if people are not excited about your mission statement, your organization or family will begin to lose its way. As the Bible says, "Where there is no vision, the people perish" (Proverbs 29:18 KJV). In other words, without guidance from God, law and order disappear. Without vision, the people perish.

Your Picture of the Future

The second element of a compelling vision is your picture of the future, of where you are going. What will the future look like for your team or organization if things run according to your plan?

Jesus outlined His picture of the future for His disciples when He charged them, "Therefore go and make disciples of all nations, baptizing them in the name of the Father and of the Son and of the Holy Spirit, and teaching them to obey everything I have commanded you. And surely I am with you always, to the very end of the age" (Matthew 28:19–20).

Walt Disney's picture of the future was that guests should have the same smile on their faces when they leave the park as when they entered. After all, when you're in the happiness business, you want to keep people smiling.

The picture of the future that Doug Erickson, of Hastings Automotive in Hastings, Minnesota, had is that his business would truly honor God and that other people would grow beside him. He says, "We've held [six Lead Like Jesus] Encounters, and we continue to use the principles of Lead Like Jesus. I never saw this in my vision, but God continues to do His thing. . . . We're watching transformation. When you open the door and let God in, wild and crazy things can happen. . . . Jesus is making miracles happen here!"

Your picture of the future is what you would like to happen if you live according to your purpose and everything goes well. Do you have a clear picture of the future? What does a good job look like? What will the future look like if events unfold as planned? Providing specific answers to these questions is important both to your people and to your organization.

When Warden Burl Cain assumed leadership responsibility for the Louisiana State Penitentiary at Angola, it was known as the bloodiest prison in the country. The largest maximum-security prison in the United States, it covers an area larger than the island of Manhattan and houses more than 5,100 men whose average sentence is eighty years. Warden Cain's picture of the future was that the culture in Angola would be transformed from one of violence to one of peace. As he explained, five things were needed to accomplish his vision: decent food, good medical care, meaningful work, significant pastimes, and the opportunity for moral rehabilitation.[2] The last element required access to faith-based resources and training.

Part of a compelling vision is a view of the future that inspires passion and, when communicated, builds commitment for the long haul. As a result of Cain's vision, some of the inmates expressed the desire to become godly fathers despite their incarceration. To meet this desire, the Malachi Dads program was created. The theme of Malachi Dads is Malachi 4:6: "He will turn the hearts of the [fathers] to their children, and the hearts of the children to their [fathers]."

It is a startling fact that more than two million children in the United States have at least one parent who is incarcerated, and these children are seven times more likely than their peers to end up in prison.[3] The goal of Malachi Dads is to reverse this trend within the families of inmates.

The Malachi Dads have used Lead Like Jesus as an integral part of the leadership training element of their two-year curriculum. In 2013, Phil traveled to the prison to witness the graduation of several Malachi Dads from the New Orleans Baptist Theological Seminary. One of these men is now serving as an inmate missionary in another prison. It's amazing what can be accomplished in the lives of many when even just one leader is committed to God's vision.

At the Lead Like Jesus ministry, our picture of the future is that someday everyone, everywhere will be impacted by someone who leads like Jesus. To accomplish that, we envision the following:

1. Jesus is adopted as the role model for all leaders.
2. All people are being drawn to Jesus by the positive impact of Christians leading like Jesus.

This kind of picture of the future keeps people going when times are tough and prevents the organization from stopping short or arriving at the wrong destination.

In every picture of the future, it is important to distinguish between *goals* and *vision*. A *goal* is a specific event that, once achieved, becomes a piece of the organization's history and, as such, is superseded by a new goal. In contrast, a *vision* is an ongoing, evolving, hope-filled look into the future that excites people even though they know they will never see its complete fulfillment.

In 1961 President John F. Kennedy challenged the American people with the *goal* of putting a man on the moon and returning him home safely by the end of the decade. When the moon landing was accomplished, NASA lost its purpose until it established a new goal.

In 1963 Dr. Martin Luther King Jr. challenged America to pursue a *vision* in his "I Have a Dream" speech. He painted a verbal picture of a spiritually transformed nation. More than forty years after his assassination, Dr. King's vision continues to stir passion and commitment.

Throughout His ministry, Jesus continually talked about the kingdom of God—its values, teachings, parables, miracles, and final fulfillment. He gave the disciples a clear picture of the future, and they committed themselves to that future—just as Christians do today.

Your Values

The third element of a compelling vision is values—those intangibles that will guide your journey and govern how you want people to behave in your organization. From our experience, very few organizations around the world have clearly defined values written down for their members.

Many companies that have spelled out their values either have too many values or do not have their values ranked. Why is it important to state and prioritize your values? Because when conflicts arise, people need to know which values are most important. Without guidelines, people do their own prioritizing, and that may lead them away from fulfilling the desired organizational purpose and picture of the future.

As we identify and prioritize our own values, it is important to know and understand what Jesus set before us as His nonnegotiable priorities. When, for instance, the Pharisees sought to test Jesus with the question "Teacher, which is the greatest commandment in the Law?" Jesus replied, "'Love the Lord your God with all your heart and with all your soul and with all your mind.' This is the first and greatest commandment. And the second is like it: 'Love your neighbor as yourself.' All the Law and the Prophets hang on these two commandments" (Matthew 22:36–40).

Notice that Jesus rank-ordered two values:

1. Love God with all your heart, soul, and mind.
2. Love your neighbor as yourself.

Even if they are rank-ordered, however, values will not drive the accomplishment of a purpose or picture of the future unless they are translated into behaviors. That's what Jesus did throughout His three-year public ministry. Clarifying how values are lived out in behavioral terms allows for accountability and the measurement of progress.

Walt Disney seemed to sense the importance of having only a few values and rank-ordering them when he prioritized his organization's four operating values, which Disney identifies as its "quality standards": safety, courtesy, the show, and efficiency.[4] Most people, when they think about Disney, would probably put courtesy as the number one value, followed by efficiency, because they think that making money would be next in importance. Then safety might be third and the show, fourth.

Actually, Disney's first priority is safety. "Ahead of courtesy?"

you ask. Yes, because leaders realized that if guests were to leave the park on a stretcher, they would not have the same smiles on their faces leaving the park as they had when entering the park. When you reflect on the fact that Disney employees are in the happiness business, this ranking makes sense.

Imagine that a cast member (Disney employee) is enjoying a conversation with a guest when they hear a scream. To follow Disney's values, the cast member will excuse himself immediately and focus on the number one value—safety. If these values were not rank-ordered, the cast member might say, "People are always yelling in the park," and then continue talking to the guest. A manager might confront the cast member by saying, "You were closest to the scream. Why didn't you react?" The cast member could respond, "I was being courteous." Cast members know that safety takes precedence over courtesy.

Why is it important to know that efficiency—having a well-run and profitable organization—is ranked fourth? First of all, it indicates that efficiency is indeed a value. But, second, because it is ranked fourth, Disney employees who are following their company's values will do nothing to save money if it compromises safety, courtesy, or the show. These three values are all ranked higher than efficiency.

At the Lead Like Jesus ministry, we have established these as our rank-ordered values:

1. Glorify God in all we do.
2. Honor Jesus as the greatest leadership role model of all time.
3. Build relationships based on trust and respect.
4. Create biblically sound content and teaching.
5. Practice wise stewardship of time, talent, treasure, and influence.

Then each of these values is operationally defined. For example, we will know that we are *glorifying God in all we do* when we do the following:

- Give God all the credit.
- Relinquish all problems to His care.
- Seek His face by worshiping together, studying together, and praying together.
- Love one another as He loves us: we are loving truth tellers, honoring one another's commitment to the Lord and encouraging one another's spiritual health and well-being.
- Express love to one another through our patience, kindness, generosity, courtesy, humility, good temper, guilelessness, and sincerity.
- Proceed boldly in living the Lead Like Jesus message in our personal and professional lives.

True success in leadership depends on how clearly the organization's values are defined, ordered, and lived out by the leader.

Everyone is watching. If leaders live their values, then others are ready to follow suit. Jesus lived His values of love of God and love of His neighbor all the way to the cross: "Greater love has no one than this: to lay down one's life for one's friends" (John 15:13).

PAUSE AND REFLECT

Imagine you were being interviewed by your ten-year-old daughter, and she asked you the following questions:

- "Why are we called a family?"
- "If we were considered a really good family, how could we tell?"
- "What are the four most important values in our family?"

What would your answers be?

MAKING TOUGH VALUE CHOICES

Many of us work in organizations that have established—either intentionally or by default—a set of operating values. Conflicts between these organizational values and someone's personal values are a reality. What do you do when the values of the organization do not align with your own? You may realize this only over time as you notice gaps between the established purpose and values and what is acted out on a day-to-day basis. You are faced with a choice: you can stay and compromise your values, you can stay and seek to be an active influence for change in the organization, or you can leave.

Leading like Jesus means not letting the organization change your values or force you to compromise them. If the temptation to compromise your values does arise, it is likely to stem from EGO issues—particularly toxic fears, such as fear of rejection, fear of poverty, fear of ridicule, fear of confrontation, or fear of lost position. Jesus dealt with this dynamic of choice when He spoke of the impossibility of serving two masters at the same time: "No one can serve two masters. Either you will hate the one and love the other, or you will be devoted to the one and despise the other. You cannot serve both God and money" (Luke 16:13).

Jesus posed the ultimate challenge for His followers when He spelled out the long-range price of compromise: "What good is it for someone to gain the whole world, and yet lose or forfeit their very self?" (Luke 9:25). Jesus also told us that we can trust in His promise never to leave us alone or outside the range of His care and concern for us.

Leading like Jesus means you may have to make a choice to be an agent of change or to seek an environment more aligned with your values. The appropriate response for your circumstances will depend on what God has in mind for you.

Life and leadership are all about choices. Choices are made based on your values. You are in fact a monument to the choices you have made over the course of your life. If you want to change your life, embrace the values of Jesus, the Servant Leader.

ESTABLISHING GOALS

Once your vision is set, you can then establish goals to answer the question *What do you want people to focus on now?* A compelling vision gives goals real significance.

As we said earlier, don't have more than three to five main goals. This way you will be able to focus on the goals you think will make the biggest difference in fulfilling your vision.

An important part of goal setting is making sure everyone knows what good behavior looks like. Anyone who has attempted to get a teenager to pick up his or her room knows the general instruction "Clean up your room" is not effective. When you go back two hours later, the teen is standing proudly in the middle of a four-foot-square clean zone surrounded by undisturbed chaos, claiming proudly to have done what you asked.

Sometimes in the haste of the moment, leaders conclude for the sake of personal convenience that they have been perfectly clear about what they want in their initial instructions, and then hold their listeners accountable for perfect comprehension, perfect retention, and perfect execution. Serving people well as a leader means testing for understanding—and repetition, repetition, repetition. Great leaders almost become like third-grade teachers.[5] They communicate their vision, values, and goals over and over and over again until people get them right, right, right!

PAUSE AND REFLECT

What's your purpose? What is your preferred picture of the future? What are your values? What are your goals? If you can't answer those questions, you don't have a clear vision. Without a clear vision, the rest of your leadership skill and effort won't matter.

As a leader, if you cut people loose without specific directions and well-understood guidelines, they will lose their way and the organization will suffer. Guidelines are boundaries that—like riverbanks—channel energy in a certain direction.[6] If you take away the banks, there won't be a river anymore; there will be a large puddle, devoid of momentum and direction. What keeps the river flowing are its banks.

20

IMPLEMENTING YOUR COMPELLING VISION

Jesus replied, "Let us go somewhere else—to the nearby villages—so I can preach there also. That is why I have come."

Mark 1:38

The traditional pyramid hierarchy is effective for the visionary aspect of leadership. People look to the leader for both vision and direction. As the following diagram suggests, although the leader may involve experienced people in shaping direction, the ultimate *responsibility* for establishing a compelling vision remains with the leader and cannot be delegated. Once the vision is set, the rest of the organization is expected to be *responsive* to the vision, to live according to its guidelines.

Visionary/Direction Role

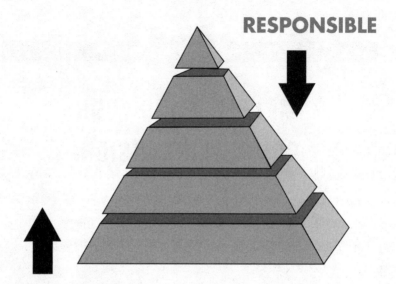

RESPONSIBLE

RESPONSIVE

As soon as people clearly understand where you want to take them and why, the emphasis switches to the second role of leadership: implementation. As the leader, you now become, in a sense, a servant of the vision: you serve the people you lead, the people whom you have asked to act according to the vision and to accomplish the stated goals.

When the leader becomes the servant, as the following diagram suggests, the traditional pyramid hierarchy must be turned upside down so the frontline people who are closest to the customers are at the top, where they can be *responsible*—able to respond—to their customers. In this scenario, leaders serve: leaders are responsive to their people's needs, training and developing them to accomplish established goals and live according to their vision of the customer experience.

Implementation Role

RESPONSIBLE

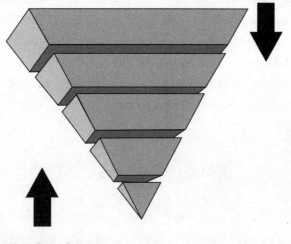

RESPONSIVE

When Jesus washed the feet of His disciples, He was transitioning His focus from the visionary or *leadership* role to the implementation or *servant* role. He turned the organizational pyramid upside down. In the process, He demonstrated the true essence of great leadership and challenged His disciples to do the same.

When we talk with leaders and managers about being a serving leader, they often are concerned about losing their positional power. Notice what Jesus said to His disciples after He had washed their feet. Jesus reclined at the table and said this to them:

"Do you understand what I have done for you?" he asked them. "You call me 'Teacher' and 'Lord,' and rightly so, for this is what I am. Now that I, your Lord and Teacher, have washed your feet, you also should wash one another's feet. I have set you an example that you should do as I have done for you." (John 13:12–15)

Did Jesus imply here that He had lost His positional power? Absolutely not. As a Jesus-like leader or manager, you still maintain your power, but your effectiveness soars because you are responding to the needs of your people. Unfortunately, some managers—in churches as well as businesses—fail to respond because they are more interested in protecting their positions than in serving others.

PAUSE AND REFLECT

What an experience that must have been for the disciples as their Lord and Teacher humbled Himself and performed such a personal and intimate act of service! Imagine being one of the disciples: having Jesus wash your feet would have been powerful and humbling.

Now think of your own life. When did someone you know perform an act of humble leadership? What was the act? What were your thoughts and feelings as you witnessed this?

As the ultimate Servant Leader, Jesus gave His disciples clear direction before He sent them out to serve. The vision Jesus cast was clear, and He had heard it from the top of the hierarchy— His Father. As fishers of men, the disciples were to "go and make disciples of all nations," focusing first on loving God and then on loving their neighbors (Matthew 4:19 ESV; 28:19; 22:37–40). And when it came to implementing this vision, Jesus wanted the disciples to be servant leaders who helped others understand and believe the good news that Jesus came to earth, lived, died, was resurrected, lives in us, and is coming again.

The implementation stage of effective leadership is where most leaders and organizations get in trouble. They keep the traditional hierarchical pyramid alive and well, but then all the energy moves away from the customers, up the hierarchy, because people feel they must please their bosses. The neglected customers are at the bottom of the pyramid. In an organization like this, as we have said earlier, self-serving leaders assume that the sheep are there for the benefit of the shepherds. Jesus spoke against this authoritarian hierarchy when He said, "Not so with you. Instead, whoever wants to become great among you must be your servant" (Matthew 20:26).

If you don't turn the pyramid upside down when you start implementing the vision, you end up with a duck pond. When there is conflict between what the customer wants and what the boss wants, the boss wins. You have people responding to customers like ducks: "It's our policy." *(Quack, quack.)* "Don't blame me; I just work here." *(Quack, quack.)* "Would you like to speak to my supervisor?" *(Quack, quack.)* But when the frontline customer contact people are treated as responsible owners of the vision, they soar like eagles rather than quack like ducks.

Jesus was often confronted with quacking Pharisees and synagogue leaders, who were more interested in protecting rules and regulations than in hearing Jesus' message of love, grace, and forgiveness. Consider this interaction:

On a Sabbath Jesus was teaching in one of the synagogues, and a woman was there who had been crippled by a spirit for eighteen years. She was bent over and could not straighten up at all. When

Jesus saw her, he called her forward and said to her, "Woman, you are set free from your infirmity." Then he put his hands on her, and immediately she straightened up and praised God.

Indignant because Jesus had healed on the Sabbath, the synagogue leader said to the people, "There are six days for work. So come and be healed on those days, not on the Sabbath."

The Lord answered him, "You hypocrites! Doesn't each of you on the Sabbath untie your ox or donkey from the stall and lead it out to give it water? Then should not this woman, a daughter of Abraham, whom Satan has kept bound for eighteen long years, be set free on the Sabbath day from what bound her?"

When he said this, all his opponents were humiliated, but the people were delighted with all the wonderful things he was doing. (Luke 13:10–17)

If you desire to lead like Jesus, being a great servant leader is crucial during implementation, when your job is to be *responsive* to your people and to help them live according to the team or organization's vision, accomplish its goals, and take care of its customers.

APPLICATION BEYOND FORMAL ORGANIZATIONS

While we have focused on the two roles of great leadership in a formal organizational context, we want to be clear that these same two aspects of leadership play out in your life role leadership position in your family, church, or volunteer organization. For example, in a family, the parents are responsible for setting the vision and establishing the goals for the family. As the kids get older, they can become involved in this process, but initially and ultimately it is the parents' responsibility to provide the visionary aspect of great leadership.

Unfortunately, many parents do not focus much attention on defining a compelling vision for their family that every member can understand. As a result, kids learn more about what *not* to do than about how to do the right thing in the right way. A great source of frustration in families is what we call *bring-me-a-rock syndrome*. It occurs when parents issue a nonspecific instruction like "Bring me a rock" but fail to test for understanding, and then become annoyed when the results don't meet their expectations. Implementation can only be effective if the important visionary work and goal setting are done first and communicated clearly. Only then can parents move to the bottom of the hierarchy and serve the family as, together, they pursue the vision.

For those who follow Jesus of Nazareth, the command for each and every person has been established by the Father and clearly communicated to all His children: "Love the Lord your God with all your heart and with all your soul and with all your mind and with all your strength" and "Love your neighbor as yourself" (Mark 12:30–31).

In the realm of family relationships, leading like Jesus means your vision is committed service in the best interest of every family member. Committed service does not selfishly exploit a person's weaknesses and shortcomings but seeks to encourage the best in each member of the family.

THE VISION OF GREAT LEADERSHIP

When Ken was a college professor, he would be in trouble with the faculty when he gave out the final exam questions on the first day of class—and he did so every semester. When the faculty found out, they asked Ken, "What are you doing?"

He calmly responded, "I thought we were supposed to teach these students."

"We are—but we don't give them the final exam ahead of time!"

Ken continued: "Not only will I give them the final exam ahead of time, but throughout the semester I'll teach them the answers to the exam questions so that when they get to the final, they'll get As."

Ken still feels strongly that life is about helping people get As, not forcing them into a normal distribution curve. Did Jesus believe in a normal distribution curve? Absolutely not! In the Great Commission, when He sent His disciples out into the world, He said to them, "Make disciples of all nations" (Matthew 28:19). He wanted everyone to become part of God's family.

Bob Buford, founder of Leadership Network and author of the book *Halftime*, believes that all of us who name Jesus as Lord are going to face a "final exam" when we stand before God at the end of our lives. According to Buford, the two questions on God's final exam will be *What did you do with Jesus?* and *What did you do with the resources you were given in life?*[1]

When you know the questions ahead of time, there is no excuse not to get an A. Most teachers have their students guess what will be on the final exam. Not so with Jesus. He was clear about the final exam and ready to help His followers get the right answers. He wants everyone to get an A.

Jesus said, "The Son of Man did not come to be served, but to serve" (Matthew 20:28). What did He come to serve? Jesus came to serve the people and prepare them to go out and share the news of forgiveness and salvation.

Chuck Colson, founder of Prison Fellowship, once preceded Ken at a conference and pointed out in his speech, "All the kings and queens in history sent their people out to die for them. I only know one King who decided to die for His people." And dying on our behalf is the ultimate in servant leadership. Jesus isn't asking us to literally die for people, but He is saying, "Not so with you," regarding the world's traditional leadership (Matthew 20:26). Jesus mandates that we establish clear visions for our organizations, visions that will in one way or another shine His light into this dark world.

The vision has to be something bigger than you, bigger than the company, the organization, or the church. Once that vision is defined, the Lord mandates servant leadership that helps people live according to that vision.

When we put the *heart* and the *head* together in a Lead Like Jesus perspective, other people become more important to us, and we take a backseat. Jesus knew His people intimately, and He equipped them to be competent and confident servant leaders. Jesus was also the preeminent spokesperson for God's vision—the purpose, the picture of the future, and the values that God created us to live out and fulfill. Turning a vision into reality requires leaders who have servant hearts and a strategy for both developing and empowering others to live according to the Lord's established vision, values, and goals.

Jesus was clear about why He came (to die on the cross as payment for our sins), what the good news was (Jesus defeated sin and death: we can be forgiven and enjoy eternal life with Him), and what He wanted people to do (name Jesus as Savior and Lord—and then share the news of His victory, His love, and His promises). Jesus also modeled great leadership—servant leadership—that others may benefit from, learn from, and emulate.

PAUSE AND REFLECT

Think for a moment about how well you serve those around you. Do you help your people pass the final exam? Do you help them live according to the Lord's, the church's, the organization's, or the company's vision? Leadership is not about power. It's not about control. It's about helping people live according to the vision.

Now we are ready to address the next domain of great leadership. We will examine the *hands*—the public leadership behavior—of a great leader in the next section.

PART V

THE HANDS OF A GREAT LEADER

"Whoever wants to be first must be your slave—just as
the Son of Man did not come to be served, but to serve,
and to give his life as a ransom for many."

Matthew 20:27–28

We believe great leadership—*servant* leadership—is an inside-out
job that begins with this key question: *Are you here on earth to
serve or to be served?* Answering this question involves your *head*:
in your mind you formulate your beliefs about leadership. However,
people won't have a clue what those beliefs are until you start to *do*
something.

GREAT LEADERS INSPIRE
GREATNESS IN OTHERS

Hands provide a powerful symbol of the *doing* aspect of leading like
Jesus. The Bible is filled with vivid images of Jesus' hands at work.
With His hands, Jesus healed the sick, cleansed lepers, fed the hun-
gry, overturned the tables of the money changers, washed the feet

of His closest disciples, and hung from a cross to save sinful human beings. With His hands, Jesus rescued the fearful, reassured the doubting, restored the fallen, and beckoned the already occupied to a higher calling and a special personal relationship with Him.

As varied as the work of Jesus' hands was, it was always motivated by the same purpose: to point people to the holy and loving God; to help them recognize their sin; and to encourage them to name Jesus as their Savior and Lord, to know His love, His forgiveness, and eternal life. Jesus' servant leadership was grounded in the grace He extended to those He called to follow Him. He accepted people where they were, regardless of their past behavior and their sin. He committed Himself to their spiritual growth and the fulfillment of their highest purpose. As Jesus glorified God in His life, He got His hands dirty. In fact, He went beyond merely proclaiming what others should do to yield to God as Lord, to die to self, and to serve others; He demonstrated with His very life His willingness to serve.

At the end of His season of earthly leadership, Jesus summed up the work of His hands in His prayer to His Father: "I have brought you glory on earth by finishing the work you gave me to do" (John 17:4). That work included teaching His disciples His message of grace, forgiveness, hope, and eternal life until they fully understood; protecting them from both external dangers and internal weaknesses; promoting unity and loving community; and preparing and equipping them to continue the work that He began in them.

In the next section we will show you how to become the servant leader Jesus wants you to be: you will learn what it takes to be a performance coach who produces great results and helps others find great human satisfaction. What distinguishes leading like Jesus from the philosophies of other performance management systems you might follow is the focus on helping people you interact with at home, at work, and in your community know the very real love of Jesus.

21

THE LEADER AS A PERFORMANCE COACH

[Jesus] said to [Simon and Andrew], "Follow me, and I will make you fishers of men."

Matthew 4:19 ESV

An effective Jesus-like leader acts as a performance coach. An essential duty of servant leaders is their ongoing investment in the lives of their followers.

Jesus was the preeminent performance coach, and He changed His leadership style appropriately as His disciples developed individually and as a group. When Jesus called His disciples to follow Him, He pledged them His full support and guidance as they became fishers of men. Jesus also empowered His followers to carry on the work of sharing the salvation message after He was gone. Through His *hands*—His effectiveness as a Servant Leader—Jesus was able to communicate to His disciples what was in His *heart* and His *head* about servant leadership.

So what does being a performance coach involve? These are the three basic components: performance planning, day-to-day coaching, and performance evaluation. Performance planning is the *leadership* aspect of servant leadership: providing direction and setting goals. Day-to-day coaching focuses on the *servant* aspect of servant leadership. That involves helping people win—accomplish their goals—by observing their performance, praising their progress, and redirecting their efforts when necessary. The third part of performance coaching is *performance evaluation*: servant leaders sit down with people and evaluate their performance over time.

Which of these three leadership activities do you think gets most of a manager's attention? Most people guess performance evaluation—and, sadly, that is the truth.

Yet performance evaluation is often a flawed practice. If leaders rate all their people high, they would be accused of being too easy, and they themselves would be rated low. As a result, the normal distribution curve is alive and well. Managers are expected to rate only a few people high, a few people low, and the rest as average performers. When we ask managers, "How many of you go out and hire losers so you can fill the low spots?" everyone laughs. Of course leaders hire either winners—people who already have a good track record in what the managers want them to do—or potential winners—people who the managers think can become winners with proper coaching. Managers don't hire losers. Why, then, do leaders have to give a certain number of people low ratings?

In Ken's teaching example, *performance planning* means giving people the final exam ahead of time. In this goal-setting stage of performance coaching, the traditional hierarchical pyramid can stay upright: if there is a disagreement over goals, the leader wins because he or she represents the organizational goals.

When Moses went to the top of the mountain to get the Ten Commandments, he didn't take a committee with him. Otherwise, he would have come down with three commandments and seven suggestions. Similarly, Jesus didn't involve His disciples much in formulating the goals He came to accomplish. He had received those from the top of the organizational hierarchy—from His Father.

These two examples, however, do not mean that in our work in the home, community, and office we shouldn't involve others in setting goals. You certainly can collaborate at work, with experienced people, and at home when the kids get older. When goals are established, though, the organizational or life role leader is responsible for making sure the direction is clear. In their life role leadership in a family, parents have to take responsibility for setting goals and objectives. We all remember times when we would say to our mothers, "All the other kids are doing it." If your mother was like Ken's, her response was always quick: "That's because their name isn't Blanchard." Our parents were in charge of performance planning for us, their kids.

We can't emphasize enough the importance of clarity of purpose in the performance planning role of a servant leader. If there is not clear communication of what a good job will look like when it is accomplished, somebody will end up frustrated—the leader, the follower, or both.

Some organizations do a good job of performance planning. Unfortunately, after goals are set and distributed, they often are filed away and forgotten until it's time for managers to evaluate their people's performances. Then everyone runs around frantically, trying to find the goals. To avoid this situation, leaders must engage in the most important element of servant leadership—*day-to-day coaching*—in which servant leaders help people reach their goals.

PAUSE AND REFLECT

Think back to a time when you were involved in a failure in communication resulting in a vast difference between what was expected and what was delivered. Recall the frustration and wasted energy that could have been avoided by initially testing for understanding.

When it comes to *day-to-day coaching*, the pyramidal hierarchy turns upside down, and servant leaders begin to work for their people. Now that the goals are clear, this aspect of being a performance coach is about teaching people the right answers—in other words, helping them accomplish their goals—so that when they get their performance review, it really will be a review. This principle also holds true in the family: after family goals are established and communicated, parents can serve their kids by being their cheerleaders, encouragers, and supporters as they work to accomplish their goals.

Whether organizational or life role leaders, servant leaders are all about helping people get As. Servant leaders aren't threatened by people around them who perform well, because their confidence is secure in the unconditional love of God. Being rooted in God's love permits servant leaders to see and respond to the success of others in a different way: they celebrate it rather than fear it.

A perfect example of someone who helps people get As is Garry Ridge, president and CEO of WD-40 Company. After Garry heard about Ken giving his students the final exam questions at the beginning of the semester, he decided to implement the "Don't Mark My Paper; Help Me Get an A" philosophy for his company's performance review system, because that philosophy aligned with Garry's beliefs about leading and motivating people.

At WD-40, every manager meets with each direct report annually to discuss the essential responsibilities set forth in that person's job description. Their discussion begins with the question "Is this still what you understand your job to be?" Once both parties are clear on the essential functions of the job, they work together to establish three to five observable, measurable goals for the coming year. This partnership aligns and clarifies expectations for both parties. Next comes day-to-day coaching—a key step in the process. The leaders continually diagnose their direct reports' development level for each goal and adjust their leadership styles to ensure they are giving the direct reports the appropriate amount of direction and support. If people attain their goals at the end of the year and live the company values as they do so, they will get an A.

When managers have come to Garry to tell him someone isn't working out and needs to be fired, Garry's first question is "What did you do to help that person get an A?" If the manager can't document the "Don't Mark My Paper" process, it's likely that Garry will fire the manager rather than the direct report. He has had to do that only a few times. Now managers all understand that their major role at WD-40 is to help people get As. Not only do the direct reports win, but so do the managers and the company.

Has this kind of performance planning and day-to-day coaching made a difference? In the last several years, WD-40 has had the highest stock price in company history. In its most recent employee satisfaction survey, filled out by 98 percent of the employees, the highest-rated statement was "I am proud to tell people I work for WD-40." Do you think the employees respond that way just because of their job responsibilities, or is it because they are in a work environment that makes people feel good about being involved? What a great example of how to achieve both great results and human satisfaction!

PAUSE AND REFLECT

In this chapter, the emphasis has been on helping people become high performers. But leading like Jesus is much more than that. To Jesus, getting an A is beyond *doing* or performing. It is about *being* a person who models His character by serving others from a loving heart yielded to Him.

Read 1 Corinthians 13 and reflect on *doing* without *being*. The math is pretty simple: Everything – Love = Nothing!

THE WORK OF THE CARPENTER

"Isn't this the carpenter's son? Isn't his mother's name Mary, and aren't his brothers James, Joseph, Simon and Judas?"

Matthew 13:55

Nothing about the life of Jesus was random or purposeless. His birth, death, and resurrection fulfilled messianic prophecy and thereby testified to a divine and perfectly executed plan. And, as with every aspect of His life, it was not by chance that Jesus spent thirty years in obscurity, learning all that God wanted Him to know while working as a carpenter. Evangelist Henry Drummond said, "What was Jesus doing in the carpenter's shop? Practicing."[1]

What was the significance of this season of practice and preparation? In what ways did working as a carpenter help prepare Jesus for His role as Messiah and, among other roles, performance coach?

We sought similarities between the work of a good carpenter and the work of a good leader, similarities that we could learn from and apply to our own leadership. Here is what we discovered:

- *Good carpenters and good leaders must be able to envision something that does not yet exist and then commit to do what it takes to create it.* Good leaders must have a compelling vision that they are passionate about and that provides direction for those who follow.

  Application: Have you established a clear direction for your people? Do they understand what business the company is in (the purpose), where it is headed (the picture of the future), and what will guide the journey (the organization's values)? Have you established goals? Have you communicated clearly enough that people know what to focus on right now?

- *Good carpenters and good leaders must be good judges of raw material.*

  Application: The raw materials of leadership are people; therefore, good leaders must be able to assess both the current condition and the future potential of their people. How well do you know the people you lead? When was the last time you consciously updated your knowledge of them? It is easy and often convenient to operate under outdated assumptions about people, to instead focus time and energy on immediate concerns despite their short-term results. Investing regularly in your people, however, will have long-term positive results.

  Also, the longer you rely on assumptions about people, the more prone you are to becoming isolated from the truth about them and ineffective in your leadership. What are some of the assumptions you have that, if inaccurate, could harm your working relationship?

- *Good carpenters and good leaders must consider the cost before the work begins.* Good leaders are realistic about the price of success, and they themselves must be willing to pay it, in full, before asking others to do the same.

Application: Jesus never downplayed the cost of following His leadership: He talked about dying to self, picking up a cross, and being persecuted. In His own acts of sacrifice and obedience, Jesus demonstrated His willingness to pay the price. Good leaders never ask anyone to do something they are not willing to do themselves.

- *Good carpenters and good leaders have a carefully defined plan for producing specific results.* A good leader serves the mission and values of the organization by focusing the means, materials, efforts, and development of people on the achievement of a specific goal and the fulfillment of a clearly communicated purpose.

Application: The plan Jesus has for producing the highest good remains the same two thousand years after He walked this earth: transform, inspire, and equip people to go forth into the world in His name, guided in love by the Holy Spirit, to make disciples of all nations.

- *Good carpenters and good leaders apply accurate measurements and standards of success to their work.* Good leaders accept responsibility for setting standards that reflect a balance between producing practical results and building healthy relationships.

Application: For Jesus, the measurement of His success was both to glorify His Father and to obey His Father's will. Public perception of leadership performance does not tell the whole story: few would have seen a man hanging on a Roman cross as the supreme example of servant leadership. A true test of leadership, however, is the impact the leader has on the spiritual well-being of those he or she influences.

The standard to which Jesus calls all His followers in the relationships they have with one another is their relationship with Him yesterday, today, and forever: "Love one another. As I have loved you, so you must love one another" (John 13:34).

- *Good carpenters and good leaders must be able to master the use of a variety of tools and know when and how to apply them to get the best results.*

Application: A good performance coach realizes that people are not all at the same level of development. Some need a lot of direction, others need a lot of support, and still others need both direction and support.

- *Good carpenters and good leaders must be willing to be both lifelong learners and lifelong teachers.*

Application: Leaders who maintain a teachable spirit and stay alert to changing times and conditions will also maintain their effectiveness in guiding others. The resource Jesus provides to all His followers is access to the indwelling and counsel of the Holy Spirit. The challenge to all who lead in the name of Jesus is this: Are you willing to listen and learn?

- *Good carpenters and good leaders know when their work is completed.*

Application: In John 16:7 Jesus said to His disciples: "It is for your good that I am going away." Jesus knew He had completed His season of earthly leadership, and He commissioned His disciples to carry on His work.

How did Jesus' leadership of His disciples line up with these insights about carpentry and leadership? First, Jesus did indeed develop a compelling vision for His disciples that motivated them after His physical time on earth ended: "The Son of Man did not come to be served, but to serve, and to give his life as a ransom for many" (Matthew 20:28).

Second, Jesus saw beyond current credentials to the long-range potential of those He called to become fishers of men. Getting to know His people was a key element of His leadership. Although He spent time teaching crowds of people and interacting with all sorts of individuals, Jesus spent most of His time with those who would comprise the next set of leaders in the movement He inspired. The Bible tells how Jesus walked with them, ate meals with them, and got to know their strengths, their weaknesses, and their individual personalities. As Jesus learned about His followers, they learned about Him.

People are not born good carpenters or good leaders. They need someone to help them grow and develop. Jesus Himself learned carpentry skills from His earthly father, and He learned to be a Master Carpenter from His heavenly Father. He also learned leadership skills He would need to develop in His disciples—not to help them become good carpenters, but to help them become fishers of men.

Our next chapter highlights the fact that leaders are made, not born. It will help you become an even better performance coach as you learn about the variety of leadership styles Jesus used to help His disciples accomplish what He was telling them to do.

THE WAY OF THE CARPENTER

Then Jesus said to his disciples, "Whoever wants to be my disciple must deny themselves and take up their cross and follow me. For whoever wants to save their life will lose it, but whoever loses their life for me will find it."

Matthew 16:24–25

The big question people ask Lead Like Jesus is, "How do you help people get As?" In other words, how do you develop people into high performers? For the answer to that question, we can trace how Jesus transformed His disciples from untrained novices to masters/ teachers and apostles for God's kingdom. We will also consider the developmental process that Jesus surely experienced as He learned the carpenter trade from His earthly father, Joseph.

A FOCUS ON PETER

As we examine how Jesus guided His disciples from call ("Follow me, and I will make you fishers of men") to commission ("Go and make disciples of all nations, baptizing them in the name of the

Father and of the Son and of the Holy Spirit"), we will focus our attention on Jesus' interactions with Peter. In his wonderful book *Twelve Ordinary Men*,[1] John MacArthur provides a compelling case for using the relationship between Jesus and Peter as an intimate case study of the transformational journey from call to commission:

> Peter's name is mentioned in the Gospels more than any other name except Jesus. No one speaks as often as Peter, and no one is spoken to by the Lord as often as Peter. No disciple is so frequently rebuked by the Lord as Peter; and no disciple ever rebukes the Lord except Peter (Matthew 16:22). No one else confessed Christ more boldly or acknowledged His lordship more explicitly; yet no other disciple ever verbally denied Christ as forcefully or as publicly as Peter did. No one is praised and blessed by Christ the way Peter was; yet Peter was also the only one Christ ever addressed as Satan. The Lord had harsher things to say to Peter than He ever said to any of the others. All of that contributed to making him the leader Christ wanted him to be.[2]

There is another reason for focusing on Peter: we can see his transformation as we look at his own words.

At the beginning of his relationship with Jesus, Peter said, "Go away from me, Lord; I am a sinful man!" (Luke 5:8). During his apprenticeship, Peter challenged Jesus and was told, "Get behind me, Satan!" (Matthew 16:23).

Shortly after this startling incident, Peter was one of three disciples privileged to hear the audible voice of God say about Jesus, "This is my Son, whom I love; with him I am well pleased. Listen to him!" (Matthew 17:5).

After following Jesus for years, Peter said, "I don't know the man!" (Matthew 26:72).

Later in life Peter wrote: "Praise be to the God and Father of our Lord Jesus Christ! In his great mercy he has given us new birth into a living hope through the resurrection of Jesus Christ" (1 Peter 1:3).

As we observe Peter in his transformational journey with Jesus, we see not only his pride and his fears on display, but his courage and his faith as well. What we see in Peter will give us an opportunity to examine how Jesus moved him from call to commission.

THE LEADERSHIP JOURNEY FROM CALL TO COMMISSION

When Jesus first called the disciples from their ordinary occupations to become fishers of men, each brought his unique life experiences and skills to this new task—but absolutely no practical knowledge of how to fill this new role. During their three years under Jesus' leadership, the disciples were transformed from untrained novices to fully equipped, divinely inspired, and spiritually grounded leaders able to fulfill the Great Commission to go to all nations with the good news of Jesus Christ's death, resurrection, and love.

What did Jesus do to facilitate the disciples' transformation, to move them from call to commission? Although miracles were involved, the process was not miraculous. It simply entailed the perfect execution of a process familiar to leaders personally committed to accomplishing a goal through the growth and development of those they lead. We believe the experience Jesus had learning the trade of carpentry provided Him with a practical model for helping people grow and develop, a model that He used to guide the learning experience of His disciples and move them from call to commission.

As He learned the carpenter craft, Jesus probably walked through these four normal stages of learning a new task: *novice* (someone just starting out), *apprentice* (someone in training), *journeyman* (someone capable of working independently), and *master/teacher* (someone highly skilled and able to teach others). Jesus brought to His leadership a clear, firsthand understanding of the journey from dependence to independence.

THE NEEDS OF A NOVICE

Novices are just starting to perform a particular task or to work toward an assigned goal. They need basic information about what to do, how to do it, when to do it, where to do it, and why it is important. Novices come in all sizes, shapes, and attitudes, from enthusiastic beginners excited about the opportunity to reluctant recruits being forced to learn. Novices also bring different personalities and learning styles. The one thing novices all have in common is the need for a leader who welcomes them into the learning process and gives them the information they need to get started.

Consider the following two examples of novices:

An excited pupil is a fifteen-year-old girl learning to drive. The day she gets her learner's permit, she is very enthusiastic, but she has little knowledge about driving a car. She needs someone to instruct her in the correct sequence of things to do before she turns on the ignition for her first drive. She doesn't need much motivation, because she already has a positive picture of what it will be like when she can drive herself and her friends anywhere she wants to go.

A reluctant recruit is a fifty-eight-year-old man learning to use a three-legged cane after suffering a stroke. The day he meets the rehab nurse who will teach him to walk with a cane, he is filled with anger and embarrassment at having to learn to do something he has been doing all his life but now has to do in a new and unattractive way.

Both novices have to follow instructions that may be new or awkward. The teenager with a glamorized view of driving her friends to the beach the day she gets her license may be overconfident and impatient with the learning process. The stroke victim, faced with a new and unappealing view of the future, may bring resentment and frustration into the learning process. He needs someone to provide a realistic view of rehabilitation and establish the sequence and the timing of the steps involved in reaching his goal.

PAUSE AND REFLECT

Think of a time when you were an untrained novice facing a new task or role. What did you need most from someone? Did you get what you needed? If not, what was the result?

Jesus and Peter the Novice

As [Jesus] walked by the Sea of Galilee, he saw two brothers, Simon who is called Peter and Andrew his brother, casting a net into the sea; for they were fishermen. And he said to them, "Follow me, and I will make you fishers of men." Immediately they left their nets and followed him. (Matthew 4:18–20 RSV)

Jesus saw in these hardworking fishermen the raw material for the future leaders of His ministry, which He would leave in their care when His season of earthly leadership was completed. In their enthusiasm, Peter and his brother Andrew literally dropped what they were doing when Jesus called them. Although he was enthusiastic, Peter had no idea how to accomplish this new task. At this novice stage of learning, Peter and the other disciples needed Jesus to teach them about their new work, and Jesus told them what to do and how to do it. When He sent the disciples out for the first time to preach the good news, for instance, He gave them extensive basic instructions on where to go, what to say, what to do, and how to do it:

> These twelve Jesus sent out with the following instructions: "Do not go among the Gentiles or enter any town of the Samaritans. Go rather to the lost sheep of Israel. As you go, proclaim this message: 'The kingdom of heaven has come near.' Heal the sick, raise the dead, cleanse those who have leprosy, drive out demons. Freely you have received; freely give.
>
> "Do not get any gold or silver or copper to take with you in your belts—no bag for the journey or extra shirt or sandals or a staff, for the worker is worth his keep. Whatever town or village you enter, search there for some worthy person and stay at their house until you leave. As you enter the home, give it your greeting. If the home is deserving, let your peace rest on it; if it is not, let your peace return to you. . . . I am sending you out like sheep among wolves. Therefore be as shrewd as snakes and as innocent as doves." (Matthew 10:5–13, 16)

PAUSE AND REFLECT

Too often leaders in churches and other organizations set people up for failure and disillusionment when they do not

THE WAY OF THE CARPENTER

respond effectively to the needs of novices. During this orientation and learning stage, show you care by providing specific direction to new recruits. Doing so makes a powerful statement about what you value—your people.

THE NEEDS OF AN APPRENTICE

Apprentices have not yet mastered all the information and skills they need in order to work independently. They need a performance coach to set goals, provide learning opportunities, observe performance, and provide feedback in the form of praise for progress and redirection when required. Apprentices also need someone to put their progress in the right perspective so they don't become overconfident with early success or discouraged with initial failure.

At the apprentice level, the teenager learning to drive has fastened her seat belt and started the car. As she pulls out into traffic and is startled by a car that seems to come out of nowhere, she begins to cry. Her instructor should praise her for fastening her seat belt and turning on the car correctly, but he also needs her to repeat back to him how the mirrors are to be adjusted and how she must look both ways to observe the flow of traffic.

At the apprentice level, the stroke victim learning to walk with a three-legged cane starts off well enough, but then he becomes frustrated and angry at the fact that it takes him many minutes to travel a distance he could previously cover in seconds. The rehab nurse needs to praise him for what he has accomplished so far and put his rate of progress in perspective even as she directs him to continue to the other side of the room.

185

It is vital that leaders provide clear direction and information and that they do so in a caring manner. Patience is a key aspect of love in action, an aspect essential to leading people through the apprentice stage. Keep the end result in mind and let the process of praising people for nearly correct behavior complete its work.

One more thing: the quickest way to stop the learning process is for the leader to grow impatient. Be obvious about the love you have for your followers, and always let your desire to lead like Jesus direct your behavior and fuel your patience.

PAUSE AND REFLECT

Think of a time when you needed someone to push you beyond a failure or an easy early success to get to a higher level of understanding and performance. Now think of a time when you quit because nobody was around to help you step up to the next level.

Your direct reports, family members, or volunteers may experience those same feelings when they confront a task or a goal they failed at earlier.

What do these scenarios say to you about your role during this phase of training apprentices?

Jesus and Peter the Apprentice

There was a time during Peter's apprentice training when he got something very right and then followed it up with something very wrong.

In Matthew 16:13–17, we read the following account:

When Jesus came to the region of Caesarea Philippi, he asked his disciples, "Who do people say the Son of Man is?"

They replied, "Some say John the Baptist; others say Elijah; and still others, Jeremiah or one of the prophets."

"But what about you?" he asked. "Who do you say I am?"

Simon Peter answered, "You are the Messiah, the Son of the living God."

Jesus replied, "Blessed are you, Simon son of Jonah, for this was not revealed to you by flesh and blood, but by my Father in heaven."

Then, just four verses later, we read:

From that time on Jesus began to explain to his disciples that he must go to Jerusalem and suffer many things at the hands of the elders, the chief priests and the teachers of the law, and that he must be killed and on the third day be raised to life.

Peter took him aside and began to rebuke him. "Never, Lord!" he said. "This shall never happen to you!"

Jesus turned and said to Peter, "Get behind me, Satan! You are a stumbling block to me; you do not have in mind the concerns of God, but merely human concerns." (vv. 21–23)

It is interesting to note that Jesus was teaching Peter in both these instances. In the first scene the teaching came in the form of high praise for getting something right (Peter identified Jesus as the Messiah and living God) and a realistic assessment of how the achievement was accomplished: God the Father had revealed the truth. In the second incident the teaching was delivered in bold language ("Get behind me, Satan!") that highlighted the seriousness of Peter's erroneous thinking and behavior that, if repeated, would disqualify the learner. Despite the high drama of that moment of correction, Peter's learning process continued in an even more dramatic fashion six days later.

In Matthew 17:1–9 we read:

After six days Jesus took with him Peter, James and John the brother of James, and led them up a high mountain by themselves. There he was transfigured before them. His face shone like the sun, and his clothes became as white as the light. Just then there appeared before them Moses and Elijah, talking with Jesus.

Peter said to Jesus, "Lord, it is good for us to be here. If you wish, I will put up three shelters—one for you, one for Moses and one for Elijah."

While he was still speaking, a bright cloud covered them, and a voice from the cloud said, "This is my Son, whom I love; with him I am well pleased. Listen to him!"

When the disciples heard this, they fell facedown to the ground, terrified. But Jesus came and touched them. "Get up," he said. "Don't be afraid." When they looked up, they saw no one except Jesus.

As they were coming down the mountain, Jesus instructed them, "Don't tell anyone what you have seen, until the Son of Man has been raised from the dead."

There would be many more dramatic moments in Peter's transformation—tests and trials that increased his knowledge of God and strengthened his faith, and experiences that God used to make him the anointed and effective leader he became. The constant throughout this transformational process was the loving commitment of the Leader to His follower during his apprenticeship.

THE NEEDS OF A JOURNEYMAN

It is easy to assume that journeymen—people who have acquired some skills for performing a task or role—have progressed to a point where all they need from a leader is to be told when and where to apply their skills. The fact of the matter is that journeymen may periodically become cautious, lose confidence, or have a diminished sense of enthusiasm for their jobs. If ignored by inattentive leaders, journeymen may quietly drift into apathy or retreat from taking risks due to a sense of lost competence or a weakened connection to their callings.

In addition, journeymen who lose their skills or desire to perform may become disillusioned critics who poison the attitude of those working around them. Leaders who ignore the journeymen's need of appreciation, encouragement, and inspiration do so at the peril of the organization.

One example of a leader meeting the needs of a journeyman is the parent who lets the teenager regain her driving privileges after an accident that she admits she could have avoided.

Similarly, the rehab nurse is meeting the journeyman's need of encouragement when she reminds the stroke victim of how far he has come in gaining his new skill and how proud she is of him as he prepares to use his cane in front of his family and friends.

Jesus and Peter the Journeyman

Peter exhibited behaviors characteristic of a journeyman when he walked on water:

> When the disciples saw [Jesus] walking on the lake, they were terrified. "It's a ghost," they said, and cried out in fear.
>
> But Jesus immediately said to them: "Take courage! It is I. Don't be afraid."

"Lord, if it's you," Peter replied, "tell me to come to you on the water."

"Come," he said.

Then Peter got down out of the boat, walked on the water and came toward Jesus. But when he saw the wind, he was afraid and, beginning to sink, cried out, "Lord, save me!" (Matthew 14:26–30)

Peter at this moment is a great illustration of someone capable of performing the task at hand. It took a tremendous amount of faith for him to step out of the boat and onto the churning water. So often we focus on Peter's cry for help that we forget that Peter actually *did* walk on water. In fact, he is the only one besides Jesus who has ever done such a thing. Peter's problem, though, came when he took his eyes off Jesus and began to worry about the storm. When Peter's confidence moved from high to low, his already demonstrated competence sank into the water with him.

Even though Peter had demonstrated the ability to walk on water, Jesus was there to provide the support Peter needed when he started to sink: "Immediately Jesus reached out his hand and caught [Peter]. 'You of little faith,' he said, 'why did you doubt?' And when they climbed into the boat, the wind died down" (vv. 31–32).

What can we learn from the response of Jesus as Leader when Peter started to sink? First, we notice that Jesus acted immediately. He did not let Peter sink into the water and think about his mistake. Jesus let Peter know immediately that He was there to help him and support him.

Next, we observe that Jesus "reached out his hand and caught him" (v. 31). Jesus used a personal touch to save the floundering apostle. Jesus knew that Peter's primary need was support, so He used His own hand to save him. Then Jesus reinforced His continued support of Peter when He said, "You of little faith . . . why did you doubt?" (v. 31). In other words, Jesus reminded Peter—and us— that He is always there when His followers need Him.

It is also important to remember that after Jesus caught Peter, they were still outside the boat. Imagine Jesus wrapping His arms around Peter and walking him back to safety. Providing support to the people around us is key to their continual development, whether in the office, the home, or the community.

THE NEEDS OF A MASTER/TEACHER

Masters/teachers have fully developed skills as well as the confidence and motivation to independently produce excellent results; they also possess the wisdom and insight necessary to teach others. The masters/teachers you lead need to be given the opportunity and challenge to pass on what they know to the next generation of learners—and they need your blessing.

Examples of masters/teachers include the former driving student a few years later, riding along with her younger brother, who has his learner's permit, and educating him on the rules of the road; and the stroke victim, now walking on his own as he visits the rehab facility to encourage new patients who are on the same path to independence that he traveled.

PAUSE AND REFLECT

"Go and make disciples of all nations, baptizing them in the name of the Father and of the Son and of the Holy Spirit, and teaching them to obey everything I have commanded you" (Matthew 28:19–20). Commissioning followers to go and teach others is the highest form of recognition a teacher can give a student. Fulfilling the commission is the highest compliment and act of gratitude a student can give a teacher. What are you doing to pass along to the next generation that which has been given to you?

Jesus and Peter the Master/Teacher

The disciple's training was complete, but a final set of questions had to be answered before this student could be certified as a master/teacher ready to lead others in the Teacher's name. Listen to the conversation:

When they had finished eating, Jesus said to Simon Peter, "Simon son of John, do you love me more than these?"

"Yes, Lord," he said, "you know that I love you."

Jesus said, "Feed my lambs."

Again Jesus said, "Simon son of John, do you love me?"

He answered, "Yes, Lord, you know that I love you."

Jesus said, "Take care of my sheep."

The third time he said to him, "Simon son of John, do you love me?"

Peter was hurt because Jesus asked him the third time, "Do you love me?" He said, "Lord, you know all things; you know that I love you."

Jesus said, "Feed my sheep. Very truly I tell you, when you were younger you dressed yourself and went where you wanted; but when you are old you will stretch out your hands, and someone else will dress you and lead you where you do not want to go." Jesus said this to indicate the kind of death by which Peter would glorify God. Then he said to him, "Follow me!" (John 21:15–19)

PAUSE AND REFLECT

The connection between loving God and leading others in His name is irrefutable. You can't do one without the other in a way that would honor God and provide the best in both results and relationships.

On the last day of His earthly season of growing and developing His disciples, Jesus had some final instructions before sending them out in His name:

"All authority in heaven and on earth has been given to me. Therefore go and make disciples of all nations, baptizing them in the name of the Father and of the Son and of the Holy Spirit, and teaching them to obey everything I have commanded you. And surely I am with you always, to the very end of the age." (Matthew 28:18–20)

How successfully Jesus had prepared His disciples for this high calling is evident when we read about Peter spreading the good news in Acts 2:36–41:

"Therefore let all Israel be assured of this: God has made this Jesus, whom you crucified, both Lord and Messiah."

When the people heard this, they were cut to the heart and said to Peter and the other apostles, "Brothers, what shall we do?"

Peter replied, "Repent and be baptized, every one of you, in the name of Jesus Christ for the forgiveness of your sins. And you will receive the gift of the Holy Spirit. The promise is for you and your children and for all who are far off—for all whom the Lord our God will call."

With many other words he warned them; and he pleaded with them, "Save yourselves from this corrupt generation." Those who accepted his message were baptized, and about three thousand were added to their number that day.

We can look at Peter here and see how, under Jesus' mentoring, he had been moved from call to commission. He demonstrated his ability as a master/teacher when he spoke to a crowd of thousands, and three thousand people chose to be baptized that day. Peter had the knowledge he needed to effectively share the message of Jesus, and he also exhibited a high level of commitment as a master/ teacher. Notice the boldness and authority with which Peter shared the message of Jesus. He truly was a fisher of men.

PAUSE AND REFLECT

What is your desire for the people who look to you for leadership? More specifically, what do you want to be able to do for frustrated individuals who do not have the competence or commitment to accomplish an assigned task? And what do you want to do for those people who not only are able to do the task on their own but also can teach others? How can your organization most benefit from people who not only are good at doing their jobs but who also are willing and able to teach others?

Sending out someone to act on your behalf is the highest form of trust in that individual's competence and commitment. When Jesus gave the Great Commission to His disciples, He considered them masters/teachers ready to perform on their own. While Jesus would not be physically present to direct and support the disciples as He had for three years, He did not turn His back on them. He promised, "I am with you always, to the very end of the age" (Matthew 28:20).

One more comment about a master/teacher's needs. *Delegating* and *abdicating* are very different. Leaders who *abdicate* turn their backs on their now-trained people, walk away from the relationships they have established, and only become involved again if they happen to hear bad news. But leaders who *delegate* stay in the information loop and are ready to help if they are called. Jesus delegated when He issued the Great Commission, but He did not abdicate. Jesus knew His disciples would need Him in the future, and He remained ready and available to support or direct them whenever they called.

LEARNING STAGES	LEADER PROVIDES
NOVICE Someone just starting out	**INSTRUCTION** Basic information: what how, where, when, why
APPRENTICE Someone in training	**DEVELOPMENT** Instruction, practice, and evaluation
JOURNEYMAN Someone able to work on his or her own	**MENTORING** Assignment and encouragement
MASTER Someone able to teach others	**COMMISSIONING** Affirmation and autonomy

LEADER-FOLLOWER PARTNERSHIP

For individuals to advance from novice to master/teacher, as this diagram[3] illustrates, they need leadership partners who can give them whatever direction and support they need to progress to the next stage of learning. A successful learner development process depends on the mutual commitment of leader and follower.

Furthermore, we need to remember that no one is totally a novice, apprentice, journeyman, or master/teacher in all the things he or she does. For instance, at any one time in our work lives, we could actually be at all four learning stages. You could be a novice on the new computer program, an apprentice in budgeting, a journeyman when it comes to people development, and a master at planning. As a result, a leadership partner not only must learn to use *different strokes for different folks* but will probably end up using *different strokes for the same person*, according to the different aspects of their organizational development.

For a leader-follower partnership to be effective, certain things have to take place. Both leader and follower must

- understand the learning stages and the follower's needs at each stage;
- agree on goals and objectives for the follower;
- identify together the follower's learning stage for each goal;
- determine together what the follower needs at each stage for each goal and how the leader will provide it; and
- be aware when the follower is shifting to a new learning stage and what that means to their leader-follower relationship.

When leaders follow these steps, they are better able to help their people become high performers in their areas of responsibility.

PAUSE AND REFLECT

Think about these leader-follower partnership steps. Have you done anything similar to the actions listed above to help your people become high performers? If not, what can you do to begin to make your relationship with your people a true partnership? Identify the first step you want to take and decide when you will implement it.

THE EGO FACTOR

Let your conversation be always full of grace, seasoned
with salt, so that you may know how to answer everyone.

Colossians 4:6

To be an effective coach, you have to meet people where they are.
Yet, whether in the office, at home, or in the community, a servant-
hearted leader confronted with a self-focused follower faces the
twofold challenge of ministering to the heart of the follower as
well as moving the learning process along. When your leadership
is challenged or your motives and methods are mistrusted, keeping your EGO—your Edging God Out tendency—in check can be
a daunting chore. Reacting out of pride, making decisions based on
fear, or resorting to using position-driven power to exert your will
can easily shortcut the learning process.

On the other hand, a servant-hearted follower confronted with
a self-focused leader faces the challenge of being a positive witness
to the leader while continuing to acquire the skills and experience
needed to be productive and grow. It can be done, but it may be an
uphill climb. An EGO-driven leader can create disillusionment and
cynicism in even the most servant-hearted follower, resulting in an
ineffective learning process.

For a leader, the quickest remedy for the EGO factor in leader-follower relationships comes with acknowledging and combating the propensity toward pride and fear. Furthermore, the leader's spiritual health encourages a follower's trust and commitment. If you seek to inspire and equip others to attain higher standards of performance and commitment, the best first step is modeling integrity in your own journey.

For followers whose self-worth and security are grounded in God's unconditional love and promises, it is important to keep a big-picture perspective of what is to be gained or lost by responding to poor treatment by an EGO-driven leader. If both leader and follower are willing to share their vulnerabilities and support each other in keeping on track, the best of all results is possible—the true win-win-win situation. The leader wins, the follower wins, and God wins!

THE EGO FACTOR IN LEADER-FOLLOWER RELATIONSHIPS

When grace abounds, results and relationships flourish. When there is strife, results and relationships suffer. Whoever extends grace promotes grace in the lives of others, and everyone benefits.

The true test of great leadership comes when the EGO of the leader and the EGO of the follower engage one another. How well they recognize and overcome the pride and fear in their relationship will determine whether they move toward the mutual satisfaction of commonly held goals—or share in frustrations of their own making.

The following diagram is an effective tool for understanding the EGO factor in leader (L)–follower (F) relationships. When things are not going well in a relationship, the diagram can help identify potential roadblocks to unity of purpose.

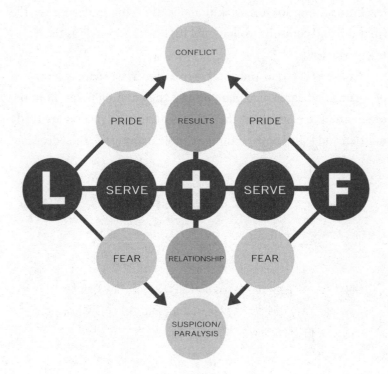

THE MOST FAVORABLE LEADER-FOLLOWER RELATIONSHIP

A Servant-Hearted Leader + A Servant-Hearted Follower = Results and Relationships

The ideal relationship between leader and follower is characterized by mutual service and trust. Creativity and learning can occur, blind spots can be uncovered, and potential misunderstandings can be avoided. This is the true win-win-win situation.

Example: A mother and teenage daughter exchange information and reach a compromise on something.

Example: After sharing different opinions about the necessary level of training for a new skill application, the leader makes the final call and commits to changing his leadership style as the training progresses.

Example: A coach and a star player discuss a situation at the end of a game and agree on a plan to score the winning point. Both the coach and the player have their EGOs under control and are ready to listen and learn; both commit to implementing the final decision.

PAUSE AND REFLECT

The ultimate example of a leader-follower relationship operating with a bond of mutual service was played out in the Garden of Gethsemane between Jesus and His Father: "My Father, if it is possible, may this cup be taken from me. Yet not as I will, but as you will" (Matthew 26:39).

FOUR LEADER-FOLLOWER RELATIONSHIPS THAT ARE ALWAYS INEFFECTIVE

Undesirable patterns occur when pride and fear commingle.

1. A Prideful Leader + A Prideful Follower = Conflict and Competition

When both leader and follower bring their pride into a relationship, a test of wills can result. Then, instead of cooperating and making concessions, the parties seek to promote their positions by winning arguments and showing off their strength.

Example: A championship coach with a ball-control strategy for winning meets a young superstar known for his brilliant individual skills.

Example: A father and son are too proud to say, "I'm sorry . . ." or "I need . . ."

2. A Fearful Leader + A Fearful Follower = Isolation and Paralysis

When a leader and a follower are both fearful, they will be looking for early warning signs that their fears are justified. Initial evidence of goodwill is looked upon with suspicion, and reluctance to share information can be a barrier to facing problems as they arise.

Example: An insecure leader who fears loss of position and a follower afraid of being taken advantage of engage in a superficial exchange of mutual compliments and guarded responses to questions about the current state of things.

3. A Prideful Leader + A Fearful Follower = Exploitation

When leaders impose their will and their way on their followers as a demonstration of their self-importance, it can play on the insecurities of the followers—leading to results that are not likely to be for the common good.

Example: A results-driven pastor intimidates his congregation into voting for a new sanctuary.

4. A Fearful Leader + A Prideful Follower = Manipulation

When an insecure leader makes unwise concessions or tries to exert position power to gain the cooperation of a strong-willed follower, the results are damaging.

Example: A micromanaging team leader who fears losing control meets a prideful journeyman who responds with malicious obedience by complying with instructions he knows are faulty.

Example: A parent who is afraid of being embarrassed by a child's temper tantrum allows the child to keep the bag of cookies taken off the shelf in a grocery store.

FOUR LEADER-FOLLOWER RELATIONSHIPS THAT CAN BE IMPROVED

Four combinations of leader and follower EGOs present specific challenges, but these relationships can be improved if one party is willing to serve as an agent of change. When that person is a leader, being the change agent is a ministry opportunity. When that person is the follower, it is a witnessing opportunity.

1. A Servant-Hearted Leader + A Fearful Follower = Ministry

A servant-hearted leader remains patient with followers who act on their insecurities: the leader offers sincere reassurance by praising progress and honest effort.

Example: A physical therapist responds with patience and encouragement to outbursts of frustration and fear by a stroke victim learning to walk with a cane.

Example: A parent is patient with a child having a temper tantrum.

2. A Servant-Hearted Leader + A Prideful Follower = Ministry

Servant-hearted leaders not only model humility and strength of purpose, but they also are willing to enforce standards and withstand challenges to their leadership.

Example: When His prideful disciples argued about who was greatest among them, Jesus responded by washing their feet.

3. A Prideful Leader + A Servant-Hearted Follower = Witness

The follower is willing to risk a negative response from the leader in order to uphold a principle or correct an error.

Example: The prophet Nathan confronted King David regarding his misconduct with Bathsheba.

4. A Fearful Leader + A Servant-Hearted Follower = Witness

A follower responds to the leader's insecurities with humility and respect without forgoing principle.

Example: While being pursued by a fear-driven King Saul, David decided not to kill him when he had the chance.

Example: A college-bound daughter is patient with a parent who is fearful about her going away to school.

THE EGO FACTOR IN THE FOUR LEARNING STAGES

As we have emphasized, we all fall short of perfection. Every day we have to confront our own EGO issues that can get us off purpose and affect the leader-follower relationship. Let's see what EGO issues leaders and followers might face at each of the four learning stages.

Novice Stage

Learner/Novice EGO Issues	Teacher/Leader EGO Issues
Fear of failure	Impatience when teaching fundamentals
Fear of inadequacy	Frustration with slow progress
Fear of looking foolish	Temptation to delegate prematurely
False pride in position	Quick judgments of learners' potential
False pride due to prior performance	Fear of failure
Lack of trust in leader or in method of training	

Apprentice Stage

Learner/Apprentice EGO Issues	Teacher/Leader EGO Issues
Discouragement with the lack of progress	Fear of failure
Impatience with the learning process	Frustration with lack of enthusiasm
Loss of faith in the learning process	Unrealistic expectations of people
Fear of failure	Fear of other people's opinions
Fear of inadequacy	Fear of criticism
Loss of faith in the leader	Fear of losing position
Diminished enthusiasm for the task	

Journeyman Stage

Learner/Journeyman EGO Issues	Teacher/Leader EGO Issues
Fear of failure when moving into new situations	Lack of sensitivity and lost enthusiasm
Fear of success in expanded use of skills	Impatience
Burnout: loss of enthusiasm and vision	Fear of the intimacy required to deal with an individual's issues
Fear of obsolescence	Fear that the learner will surpass the teacher
Fear of competition	
Fear of being confronted about slips in performance	
Fear of being exploited	

Master/Teacher Stage

Learner/Master EGO Issues	Teacher/Leader EGO Issues
Complacency with current knowledge of skills	Fear of personal competition from the completely inspired and fully equipped follower
Unwillingness to take criticism or direction	Fear of personal obsolescence when the learner can do what the teacher does
Arrogance	Unwillingness to share information or recognition
Misuse of skills for self-serving purposes	Fear of losing control

Aware of the potential EGO barriers in their relationship and willing to address them, leader and follower can seek individually and together to overcome these barriers through personal preparation, open communication, and a mutual commitment to serve one another and their relationship.

PAUSE AND REFLECT

What kind of performance coach are you? Do your people know what you expect them to accomplish? Once you are sure your goals are clearly understood, do you focus all your efforts on helping your people win, accomplish their goals, get an A? Are you able to maintain a servant's heart even though some of your people are driven by false pride or fear? Be honest.

PART VI

THE DOING HABITS

Love must be sincere. Hate what is evil; cling to what is good. Be devoted to one another in love. Honor one another above yourselves. Never be lacking in zeal, but keep your spiritual fervor, serving the Lord. Be joyful in hope, patient in affliction, faithful in prayer. Share with the Lord's people who are in need. Practice hospitality.

Romans 12:9–13

Over the last ten years we have realized that a relationship with Jesus is critical to leading like Jesus. We will not lead differently until we become different people through the transformation that results from a relationship with Jesus. We can't lead like Jesus without following Jesus. We have also come to recognize that leading like Jesus is not possible by ourselves. We just can't do it alone. Only through an intimate relationship with Jesus and experience with the habits that allow us to be with Him and focus on Him are our hearts transformed, our minds informed, and our behavior changed. What we do as leaders is a direct result of what has happened in our hearts and minds when we've spent time in the transforming presence of God.

In Part III we talked about the Being Habits of experiencing solitude, practicing prayer, knowing and applying Scripture, and maintaining supportive relationships—all practices that reinforce the central habit of accepting God's love and abiding in it.

As we have continually said, if we want to lead like Jesus, we need to become more like Jesus. When we look at Jesus not only as our Savior and Lord, but as the One whom God wants us to emulate every day, we realize that we leaders must practice certain habits. In the book of James, for instance, we are encouraged to be "doers of the word," and not merely "hearers" of it (1:22 ESV). In other words, we must move from *being* to *doing*. This shift is particularly important since we believe the next great movement in Christianity must be not just proclamation; it must be demonstration.

If we want people to believe what we believe, we must behave differently than nonbelievers do. Jesus put it this way: "In the same way, let your light shine before others, that they may see your good deeds and glorify your Father in heaven" (Matthew 5:16).

If we model our leadership after Jesus, it makes sense for us to look closely at five habits that characterized His interactions with people.

You'll notice that obeying God and expressing His love is the central Doing Habit. The other four habits—grace, forgiveness, encouragement, and community—are His people's expressions of God's unconditional love.

THE HABIT OF OBEYING GOD AND EXPRESSING HIS UNCONDITIONAL LOVE

As God's chosen people, holy and dearly loved, clothe yourselves with compassion, kindness, humility, gentleness and patience. Bear with each other and forgive one another if any of you has a grievance against someone. Forgive as the Lord forgave you. And over all these virtues put on love, which binds them all together in perfect unity.

Colossians 3:12–14

We are often asked, "What does love have to do with leadership?" The simple answer is . . . *everything.* Love is a core value of leadership, especially for a Jesus-like leader. The question in every situation where we have influence becomes, "What is the most loving thing to do?" As a leader, you always have the choice of responding in a loving way—and that option is not usually the easiest way. Sometimes love will require you to let go of your pride and fear and do the hard thing of holding a staff member accountable. Leaders sometimes shy away from those conversations, but love requires you to speak the truth in a way that helps someone move forward. There are also situations when the most loving thing to do is to set someone free. As leaders, we are to ensure that even removing people from our staff is done with grace, dignity, generosity, and, yes, love.

We also must ask, "What is the most loving thing to do?" when we are leading our families. Sometimes we are kinder, more loving, and more thoughtful to complete strangers than to the people we love most. Creating an environment of love in our homes will develop people who love. In fact, as leaders, we are to create an environment of love, grace, and thoughtfulness everywhere we have influence.

God's Word is very clear about this call to all of His followers. The concept of love appears throughout Scripture. The two greatest commandments are to love God with all that we are and to love other people as we love ourselves (Matthew 22:36–40). And in 1 Corinthians 12:31 Paul wrote, "You should earnestly desire the most helpful gifts. But now let me show you a way of life that is best of all" (NLT). He continued:

> If I could speak all the languages of earth and of angels, but didn't love others, I would only be a noisy gong or a clanging cymbal. If I had the gift of prophecy, and if I understood all of God's secret plans and possessed all knowledge, and if I had such faith that I could move mountains, but didn't love others, I would be nothing. If I gave everything I have to the poor and even sacrificed my body, I could boast about it; but if I didn't love others, I would have gained nothing. (13:1–3 NLT)

Did you get that? If we don't love, we *are* nothing and we *gain* nothing. As we have said, leading like Jesus is leadership based on love. Leading like Jesus will always mean putting love into action in various ways.

PAUSE AND REFLECT

In his book *The Greatest Thing in the World*, Henry Drummond identifies nine elements in what he calls the "spectrum of love."[1] Using 1 Corinthians 13:4–7 as his source, Drummond lists patience, kindness, generosity, courtesy, humility, unselfishness, good temper, guilelessness, and sincerity.

For those of us striving to lead like Jesus, a challenging exercise is to study these aspects of love and then ask ourselves these questions about each one:

- When do I demonstrate this aspect of love in my life?
- When do I struggle to demonstrate this aspect of love in my life?

The more insight you have into how you express these elements of love, the better you can integrate them into the day-to-day choices you make, and the more easily you can become a love-based leader.

As God's people we are "rooted and established in love" (Ephesians 3:17)—in *His* love. God loved us first, and He expressed that love by coming to this earth as Jesus, who died on the cross for our sin. That is love!

What we have received, we can give away to others. So we who have received God's love can share that love with others. And the power of God's love changes everything. The kind of love we are writing about can't come from us; it is a love that seeks a person's good even when it costs us. It is a love that is committed to helping people move from where they are to where God wants them to be. This love speaks the truth boldly and at the same time holds hands gently. How do you love like that? Again, *you* can't. But God can love people through you, when you are willing to let Him. Don't misunderstand: in some instances, no matter what you do or how much you love, people or circumstances may not change. (God gives you boundaries to protect yourself from unchanging and abusive situations.) But let us share one story of a changed life, of a life redeemed by love.

A woman in one of our Lead Like Jesus encounters told us about how she married a wonderful man, but she had no idea of the anger stored deep in his heart. It started to appear during their honeymoon with name-calling, expletives, and anger about the smallest things. She decided *she* was the problem. If she behaved differently, she reasoned, he would go back to being the person she thought she had married. She adjusted her behavior and tried to do everything to please him. The most difficult part was trying to anticipate his anger, because there was absolutely no pattern to it. On one day a certain situation would be no problem, but on another day that same situation would prompt an angry tirade. She lived on eggshells, and they were cracking. She became ill with physical conditions she had never before experienced. Doctors treated her, but she came to realize that these illnesses were her body's response to what she was experiencing in her marriage.

She prayed tirelessly for her husband. She made suggestions to him; she even tried to be the voice of God in his head—but nothing changed. One day, in complete desperation, she prayed, "Father, please help me love him like You love him. Help me see him as You do—not as who he is today, but who he will become by Your grace. Help me forgive him before he hurts me again. Help me release unforgiveness—and help me give him grace. Help me not to blame myself when he says hurtful things. Protect my heart that I might respond with love."

After that prayer she began to see her husband differently. She made sure she caught him doing things right so that she could encourage him. She reminded him of her love through notes and cards. She planned fun times she knew he would enjoy. She remembers the first time he apologized to her after an angry episode—she could hardly believe it! She felt she was watching a transformation happen before her eyes. It was a long season, but God used this woman to love her husband into the man he had always wanted to be.

Love redeems. When we receive love, we will express it to others in obedience to the One who loved us first, the One who has commanded us to love Him and love others. We will express that love through the habits of grace, forgiveness, encouragement, and community.

PAUSE AND REFLECT

Today, what can you do to more effectively reflect God's unconditional love to those around you?

THE HABIT OF GRACE

God is able to bless you abundantly, so that in all things
at all times, having all that you need, you will abound in
every good work.

2 Corinthians 9:8

We may think withholding forgiveness affects only the person we
need to forgive and ourselves. The truth, however, is that unforgiveness takes root in our hearts, and the bitterness that grows
there will affect all of our relationships. Similarly, the choice to stay
in the past instead of enjoying the present moment will also have
an impact on the people we influence. Grace and forgiveness are a
one-two punch. It's been said that forgiveness is the cake and grace
is the icing that covers over the past and the sins that have been
forgiven.

Grace has been defined as getting something you don't deserve.
We know this to be true: "It is by grace you have been saved, through
faith—and this is not from yourselves, it is the gift of God—not by
works, so that no one can boast" (Ephesians 2:8–9).

Where would we be without grace? We would all be in trouble.
Scripture calls us to "look after each other so that none of you fails

to receive the grace of God" (Hebrews 12:15 NLT). As leaders, we are dispensers of grace in our families, churches, and organizations. We can extend the grace of believing that people are doing the best they can, given their level of awareness. It is up to us to make sure grace is extended; we lead in the way of grace.

If you have ever needed grace, you know its power. Knowing you deserve judgment and punishment but receiving grace instead is hard to believe and hard to describe. Romans 5:20–21 says this about grace:

> God's law was given so that all people could see how sinful they were. But as people sinned more and more, God's wonderful grace became more abundant. So just as sin ruled over all people and brought them to death, now God's wonderful grace rules instead, giving us right standing with God and resulting in eternal life through Jesus Christ our Lord. (NLT)

It's hard to believe that as people sin more, God's grace becomes more abundant. Later in the book of Romans, the obvious question is asked and answered: "Well then, should we keep on sinning so that God can show us more and more of his wonderful grace? Of course not! Since we have died to sin, how can we continue to live in it?" (6:1–2 NLT). We are different people because of grace; we do not want to go back to being the people we were. So our response to grace is not to continue in our bad behavior, but to want to do better. Have you ever acted like a total jerk and then had someone who loves you respond with grace? Did you feel like an even bigger jerk? Ideally this kind of grace stops us—and our wrong behavior—in our tracks.

Our friend Tom told us an incredible story of grace. Early in his marriage, his wife caught him with another woman—literally. When she did, she walked up to him and said, "We will talk about this later." He rushed home to see if she would talk then, but she told him she would need time. It was Tuesday, and she said she would be ready to talk on Friday. Tom described those next days as torture. He knew that he had lost his wife and his two small children, that there was no way his wife would allow him to stay in their lives.

On Friday she told Tom she was ready to talk. Tom described the scene to us: he sat across from his wife, and she looked directly in his eyes. She said, "I've made a decision. I have decided that I will be the best wife you could ever have, I will be the best mother you could ever want for your children, and I will be the best lover you could ever imagine. Now you can decide what you are going to do."

Tom said he fell to his knees in front of his wife and sobbed. He had heard about grace his entire life, but he had never experienced it. In fact, his wife's incredible act of grace was the first time he truly understood God's grace. Tom told us he spent the next forty years trying to be the husband he wanted to be to his wife, and she spent the next forty years keeping the promises she made that day.

Grace is love in action after people mess up. Grace extends fellowship to others. God reached out to you in grace to restore your intimate relationship with Him: "While we were still sinners, Christ died for us" (Romans 5:8). Even when we walk away from Him in our sin, His grace abounds. And God's grace changes us!

During His season of leadership on this earth, Jesus constantly reached out in grace to heal people and restore relationships. To lead like Jesus, we must be agents of grace, "examples of the incredible wealth of his grace and kindness toward us" (Ephesians 2:7 NLT).

PAUSE AND REFLECT

Does someone in your family or workplace need grace—specifically, the chance to restore his or her relationship with you? If so, put down this book and go right now to be an agent of grace.

THE HABIT OF FORGIVENESS

"If you forgive other people when they sin against you, your heavenly Father will also forgive you. But if you do not forgive others their sins, your Father will not forgive your sins."

Matthew 6:14–15

Humanly speaking, forgiveness is impossible.

Probably everyone on the planet has been hurt by the actions or words of another person. The experiences of hurt come in a variety of ways, from broken trust to broken people. A partner sabotages your business; your spouse has an affair; a family member turns others against you; members of your church criticize you; a person you love is abusive; or someone injures a loved one. As followers of Jesus, we are taught we must forgive.

Let's be clear: forgiveness does not mean that you deny what happened. Someone hurt you, and that reality cannot and should not be minimized or rationalized. You can, however, extend forgiveness without excusing the act done against you. This is where God comes in. Out of the depth of your relationship with Him, you can seek to be willing to forgive. It is in this place of being willing that you can find the ability to extend forgiveness.

As leaders who are seeking to help people grow and develop, we need a healthy capacity to forgive, redirect, and move on. Leaders who are impatient for results can be quick to both judge and dismiss less-than-perfect efforts as failure, but the journey of forgiveness must start with us. Unlike Jesus, we all fall short of a 100 percent score on our journey as leaders. Sometimes we make mistakes we could have avoided. Sometimes we say or do things in the heat of the moment that we regret. If we are wrapped up in our performance and the opinions of others, we will be unable to forgive our own shortcomings, let alone anyone else's. Yet Jesus modeled His high standard for forgiveness when He cried out from the cross, "Father, forgive them, for they do not know what they are doing" (Luke 23:34).

One test of whether we have the heart attitude required to lead like Jesus is how we respond when those we lead fail to perform according to our expectations. We also need to remember that getting things nearly but not quite right is simply part of the learning process that precedes getting things exactly right on a consistent basis. That's why praising progress is such a powerful concept.

Our families are another place where we must demonstrate forgiveness. As parents, we may have to practice with our children what we preach and apologize for words we speak too quickly and in anger; we may have to ask our children for forgiveness. We continue to believe that people—even our children—are pretty quick to forgive when we admit a mistake. After all, our children already know we aren't perfect.

A powerful example of forgiveness comes from our friends Jim and Sheri. They had planned a four-day trip to celebrate Jim's birthday. They left home on Thursday and had special plans for a Friday celebration. On Friday morning when Jim checked his e-mail, he saw that his neighbor had sent him an array of photos from a party that had taken place at Jim and Sheri's home on Thursday evening. When he dialed into their home security camera system, Jim was able to replay the entire event. It seems their son, Christopher, had decided to take advantage of his parents being out of town and had invited a few friends over. The news of a party spread, and the guest list quickly expanded. Jim was extremely upset when he saw what had happened in his home.

Jim usually enjoyed a few minutes of quiet time early in the morning. This particular morning he read *Lead Your Family Like Jesus*. Jim was reminded in the book that because God has forgiven all of our sins, we must forgive others. He also read that sometimes when people make a mistake, we put them in a penalty box (like in hockey) and leave them there for a long time. He found himself wondering if he and Sheri had placed Christopher in a penalty box for the past four years.

Christopher had been through a tough season. A football injury during his senior year of high school had ruined his chances of going to the college of his choice. In the four years since then, multiple situations involving Christopher's behavior had challenged their family. He had been punished, restricted, and deprived of privileges, and he had never shown remorse for anything he had done.

Jim was praying about what to do when Sheri joined him. He told her the whole unpleasant story. Sheri wanted to leave right away, but Jim shared what he had been reading and his experience in prayer. They decided they needed to break the past cycle and react differently in this situation. Christopher needed their best response.

Jim and Sheri decided to celebrate Jim's birthday and continue to pray and think about what to do. Christopher called his parents, asking when they would be coming home. They told him they weren't sure if they would stay the entire four days since their schedule was very busy. Jim and Sheri had, in fact, decided to stay the entire time, but wanted Christopher to think each day could be the day they would return.

When Jim and Sheri arrived home, they found a spotless house. They knew Christopher must have worked hard to clean up the mess they had seen in the photos. They sat down with their son and told him they knew about everything. They told Christopher they loved him, they forgave him, and they understood it had been a tough four years. Their son's head dropped into his hands, and he sobbed and said, "I'm so sorry for everything I have put you through." This was a turning point. Jim told us they had waited and prayed for this moment. It came when he and Sheri were ready to trust in the power of forgiveness.

Forgiving is not a natural response to being hurt or disappointed. Forgiving is instead a supernatural act of a person who has surrendered self, plans, will, and life in obedience to God and who chooses to extend the kind of forgiveness he or she has received. Jesus taught forgiveness to His disciples, He practiced forgiveness with those who betrayed Him, and He willingly granted forgiveness to those people who participated in His death on the cross.

The opposite of forgiveness is judgment, and judgment is pointing out a fault with a view to condemnation. On the other hand, discernment is pointing out a fault with a view to correction and restoration. So when we withhold forgiveness, are we sincerely trying to correct or restore—or is there some benefit to us in condemning?

Let's look at what Scripture says: "Forget about deciding what's right for each other. Here's what you need to be concerned about: that you don't get in the way of someone else, making life more difficult than it already is" (Romans 14:13 THE MESSAGE). And James 4:11 adds this: "Don't speak evil against each other, dear brothers and sisters. If you criticize and judge each other, then you are criticizing and judging God's law. But your job is to obey the law, not to judge whether it applies to you" (NLT).

PAUSE AND REFLECT

In the game of hockey, when players violate the rules, they spend a specific amount of time in the penalty box before they can return to the game. Against that backdrop, spend a few minutes now and ask God to reveal to you the answers to the following questions:

- Have you put someone in your penalty box? How long has he or she been there? Is the time limit up?
- Are you still defining your life by how you have been hurt? If so, why?
- Are you in your own penalty box? Is the time limit up on the guilt you have felt? Why or why not?

Obeying God and expressing His love allows us to step out of the penalty box and forgive ourselves and others.

THE HABIT OF ENCOURAGEMENT

> May our Lord Jesus Christ himself and God our Father, who loved us and by his grace gave us eternal encouragement and good hope, encourage your hearts and strengthen you in every good deed and word.
>
> 2 Thessalonians 2:16–17

The Lord's grace and forgiveness offer us spiritual redirection. The Bible uses the word *repentance*—meaning "deciding to move in a new direction." It is important to note that Jesus' message from the beginning was His call to repent: "From that time on Jesus began to preach, 'Repent, for the kingdom of heaven has come near'" (Matthew 4:17). That is still Jesus' message today.

Encouragement completes the coaching cycle: it is your opportunity to help those you coach stay on course and not move backward. A key aspect of effective encouragement is catching people doing something right. The goal is to accentuate the positive, and Philippians 4:8 encourages us to do the same: "Whatever is true, whatever is noble, whatever is right, whatever is pure, whatever is lovely, whatever is admirable—if anything is excellent or praiseworthy—think about such things."

S. Truett Cathy, founder of Chick-fil-A, was often heard saying, "Who needs encouragement? Anyone who is breathing!" And our lives change in those moments of heartfelt encouragement. Remember moments from your own life: a supervisor recognized your work, you completed a project and heard "Great job," or someone noticed something different about you and complimented you. Encouragement changes our perspectives in a moment. Jesus consistently encouraged people with such words as "I will never leave you nor forsake you" (Hebrews 13:5 ESV), words that gave His disciples, then and now, the ability to live with hope.

Encouragement often does come through words, but so do wounds. Scripture cautions us to be careful about what we say: "The tongue has the power of life and death" (Proverbs 18:21). We know that to be true. We too often hear stories from adults who are still wounded by their mothers' words or struggling to be good enough to meet their fathers' standards. Some people had parents who never went to a game or a play even though their child was the quarterback or had the lead role. Sometimes encouragement is simply being present to cheer someone on.

Some leaders who are wounded find leading like Jesus difficult for them. We have found that people who don't feel very good about themselves have a hard time making others feel good about themselves through praise and encouragement. Encouragement comes from a heart that is secure enough to recognize the good in others and to express that recognition with words—and we know our words come out of the overflow of our hearts (Luke 6:45).

You may think encouragement is not a big deal, but the power of encouragement can quickly change someone's day—or even his or her life. The following two stories speak to the power of words and actions that encouraged and changed the direction of a person's life.

A man named Brian told us about a leader who made a difference in his life through encouragement. For years Brian had watched Ed walk through the office and greet people on a regular basis. He not only knew the vice presidents by name but also knew every member of the staff and treated each as a person of dignity. In most cases, Ed even knew the names of their children. He asked questions about their families and encouraged them in their work. One day Brian made a comment to Ed about his son being interested in going to medical school. Ed told Brian he knew someone at that school and would be happy to write a letter for his son. Given Ed's busy schedule, Brian wondered if he would actually have time to do it, but Ed wrote the letter. Brian's son was accepted, graduated with honors, came back to their hometown, and became a strong stakeholder in the community. Brian said that his son's life might not have played out this way if it had not been for a leader who encouraged the people he influenced.

Encouragement can be especially appreciated on the darkest day of a person's life. When Phyllis's second husband passed away, their family and friends came from around the country. After his memorial service, people from their church prepared dinner for all the out-of-town visitors. The sun had already set as Phyllis and her loved ones drove up the street to her home. As they rounded the corner, they saw lights. Hundreds of luminarias—sand-filled white bags with lighted candles flickering from inside—had been placed around her cul-de-sac, down her long driveway, and up her walkway, lighting her pathway home. The sight was breathtaking. Phyllis and her family and friends couldn't believe their eyes. The day's pain faded for just a moment as they looked at the beauty and felt the encouragement being shown to them. She found a card on her door from her neighbor, explaining that she had not known what to do to encourage Phyllis through this day. She decided that lighting a path to her home would remind her that God was still lighting her path for the future.

Encouragement is a powerful way to help those we influence experience the love of God. Ken says if he had one wish for the world, it would be that people would give up wanting to be right and instead focus on catching one another doing things right. As leaders who desire to lead like Jesus, we are to be distributors of encouragement.

PAUSE AND REFLECT

Think of those phrases you wish you had heard more often when you were growing up, phrases like "I love you," "Great job," "I love spending time with you," "You have a wonderful smile," "You bless me"—and spread those encouraging words to others today.

THE HABIT OF COMMUNITY

May the God who gives endurance and encouragement give you the same attitude of mind toward each other that Christ Jesus had, so that with one mind and one voice you may glorify the God and Father of our Lord Jesus Christ.

Romans 15:5–6

The Doing Habits of grace, forgiveness, and encouragement flourish when they happen in the context of a community—whether that community is your family, a support group at your church, or work groups in your professional life.

We were not meant to live life alone. God recognized that man should not be alone; He created a woman to be with him. Genesis 1:27–28 reads:

> God created mankind in his own image,
> in the image of God he created them;
> male and female he created them.

God blessed them and said to them, "Be fruitful and increase in number; fill the earth and subdue it. Rule over the fish in the sea and the birds in the sky and over every living creature that moves on the ground."

Living in community was God's idea, and He has given us instructions on how best to build that community.

One of the core themes of the Bible is the kingdom of God, a community where God is King. John Ortberg often asks, "What is the gospel that Jesus came to teach?" He then answers the question with various passages from the books of Matthew, Mark, Luke, John, and Acts, where Jesus proclaimed, "The kingdom of God has come near" (Mark 1:15). Scripture tells us to "seek first [God's] kingdom" (Matthew 6:33).

It's been said that your faith gets you to heaven, but your works bring heaven to earth. Lead Like Jesus leaders desire to bring heaven to earth in community. As leaders we are to model loving one another (John 13:34), forgiving one another (Colossians 3:13), and regarding others more highly than ourselves (Philippians 2:3–4). We are to teach and correct one another (Colossians 3:16), encourage one another (1 Thessalonians 5:11), pray for one another (James 5:16), and bear one another's burdens (Galatians 6:2). We are to be devoted to one another (Romans 12:10), kind and compassionate (Ephesians 4:32), and generous in hospitality (1 Peter 4:9) as we serve and "submit to one another out of reverence for Christ" (Ephesians 5:21). Leaders who desire to lead like Jesus will internalize God's command, "Love one another as I have loved you" (John 15:12 ESV), and teach others to do the same.

AN EXAMPLE OF DOING LIFE TOGETHER

"As iron sharpens iron, so one person sharpens another" (Proverbs 27:17).

One of the most important aspects of Phil's leadership journey has been being part of an accountability group with four other men. Some people don't like the word *accountability*, but as you will read in Phil's story, it has been a key habit for the spiritual growth and development of this group.

The men in Phil's group have become his closest male confidants in what they refer to as "doing life together." Phil recalls being invited to join the group when he was struggling through the early days of his first term as chairman of his church elder council. He had agreed to take the position at the request of the senior pastor who, to Phil's surprise, left to take a position at another church eight weeks after Phil had taken office. He felt overwhelmed by the burden of this leadership responsibility. He remembers riding his bicycle around his neighborhood at three in the morning and crying out to God that he couldn't do the job. Things at his company were tense and chaotic as well. The corporate office had decided to close the manufacturing plant where he worked, and Phil was working with local management and union officials to try to reverse the decision. All in all, he felt isolated and trapped by his commitments.

During this time Phil was asked by his predecessor, former church chairman Harle Damon, to meet him and two other men from their church for breakfast. Harle explained that the purpose of the meeting was to explore joining together in a fellowship of accountability to help one another in their Christian walk.

Phil had never been in such a group and was a little apprehensive about what it might entail. He wasn't sure he wanted to get involved in sharing with such an impressive set of men his struggles as a leader at work, at church, and at home. Nevertheless, Phil agreed to give it a try. Little did he know that accepting that hand of Christian fellowship was the beginning of one of the most cherished and enduring aspects in his walk of faith.

For twenty-five years, these men have been meeting once a week at the same restaurant in the same booth, ordering basically the same breakfast. Their routine has remained constant: someone leads a devotion, they pray at the beginning and the end of their time together, and they enjoy lots of laughter in between. What sets this experience apart from any other group of guys having breakfast are the accountability questions they ask one another.

Every six months they agree on a set of questions that each member will answer at each meeting. The questions address matters important to living out their faith in their personal relationships, at their church, and at work. Here are some of the enduring questions they have asked one another:

Since our last meeting:

1. Have you maintained a daily habit of prayer and time in God's Word? What did you learn about God . . . and about yourself?
2. Have you maintained a healthy balance between work, family, church, and personal time?
3. What one temptation plagued you in your walk with God this week? How did you handle it?
4. Have you devoted quality time to sustaining a vibrant, loving relationship with your wife?
5. Did you compromise your integrity this past week?
6. Have you treated the people in your life as the objects of God's affection, maintaining a positive, loving attitude toward them, using grace-filled speech with them, and avoiding crankiness, gossip, and grumbling?
7. Have you actively sought to maintain or improve your physical well-being through regular exercise, adequate sleep, and healthy eating?

The ground rules for the accountability discussions are these:

- All discussions are strictly confidential: absolutely nothing is to be shared with anyone outside the group.
- Advice is given only when it's requested. Try to avoid going into fix-it mode.
- No one is pressed to reveal more details than he feels comfortable sharing. No open-heart surgery is performed by the group.

As Phil recalls, "Having met together for breakfast more than eight hundred times, we have considered all that life can bring as reasons to pray for one another. These have included private temptations, marital and family issues, crises at work, leadership issues at church, illness within the group, death of loved ones, and, ultimately, the death of two men in the group. God has spoken to each of us through these times of open fellowship, and He has spoken words of encouragement, words of compassion, and words of wisdom in a way that has no parallel in my life."

One episode that stands out in Phil's mind was when he was greatly upset with his father. Phil felt his dad had let him down in a deep and personal way. After sharing his anger and frustration with the group, one of his brothers in Christ looked Phil in the eye and told him that he needed to let go of his anger and forgive his dad. As hard as it was to hear, Phil knew his friend was right and followed his suggestion. Phil's dad died two years later, and their relationship was sound and loving to the very end. It could have been a lot different if it hadn't been for the word of truth spoken to Phil by a man he knew and trusted.

PAUSE AND REFLECT

Several years ago a study was done of 237 Christian leaders who had experienced a moral failing. The purpose of the study was to determine if these cases had any common denominators. The researchers reported only one thing all these men held in common: not one of them had an accountability relationship with other men.[1]

Do you have an accountability group? If not, consider joining or starting one. Think of ways you could strengthen your relationships with the Lord and other believers by participating in this same kind of Christian fellowship.

In our organizations, churches, and families, we live in community. Jesus modeled living in community with His disciples. He established the mission and vision of the community, and He gave His disciples the picture of the future: "Go and make disciples of all nations" (Matthew 28:19).

Jesus built His disciples' trust in Him; they learned they could trust Jesus above all else. He also empowered the disciples, and community was built. Organizations thrive when people not only trust leadership but also feel trusted and empowered by leadership. Mutual trust is the foundation of a healthy community, but it can only develop over time.

A great example of community building in an organization is Cardone Industries, a remanufacturer of auto parts. These are the values of Cardone Industries: honor God in all we do; help people develop; pursue excellence; and grow profitably. Owner and principal Michael Cardone is a Lead Like Jesus board member. When we asked him how he integrated the values of Cardone into a multicultural, six-thousand-member workforce, he replied, "They can't argue with love." He continued, "When people know you care about them and want to help them develop, they work at a different level." We agree with Michael: love is a key element in the creation of a trusting community.

PAUSE AND REFLECT

Think of three words that describe the current culture in the community of your family, your workplace, or your organization. Are you satisfied with what these words say about your community? If not, what in your community needs to be changed?

What can you do to live out in your family, workplace, and community Jesus' command that we love one another as He has loved us? List three specific ways—and put them into action today.

A loving community sets boundaries and communicates expectations about what is acceptable within its culture and what is not. At the same time, community inspires creativity in its members. The culture of your community will therefore help determine how successfully your organization fulfills its vision and mission. Leading like Jesus calls for building a trusting and loving community. If you don't love your mission, vision, and values as well as your people and the customers you serve, you'll never get lasting results.

PAUSE AND REFLECT

Like the Being Habits, the Doing Habits can give us a sense of how ready we are to lead like Jesus today. What do your answers to these questions tell you?

- Obeying God and expressing His unconditional love—Are you willing to share God's love with those in your spheres of influence?
- Grace—Will you look for opportunities to extend grace to people at your home and workplace?
- Forgiveness—Who in your spheres of influence needs your forgiveness? When will you be able to offer it?
- Encouragement—What words of encouragement or praise can you offer someone today?
- Community—What steps can you take to foster a community of love and grace in your home and workplace?

LEADING LIKE
JESUS BEGINS IN YOU

"Therefore go and make disciples of all nations, baptizing
them in the name of the Father and of the Son and of the
Holy Spirit, and teaching them to obey everything I have
commanded you."

Matthew 28:19–20

By reading this book, you have taken the first step of an exciting
new journey to lead like Jesus. As you begin to apply what you have
learned at work, at home, or in the community, the landscape will
look familiar. The roles, responsibilities, and challenges in your life
probably have not changed since you started the book. What *has*
changed, however, is how you approach them.

The people you are around will more than likely be the same
people you were around before you started this journey. Expect
them to behave just as they have in the past and to respond to your
leadership as they always have. As they sense a change in how you
are treating them, they will, at times, question your motivations,
misinterpret what you are trying to accomplish, and test your commitment. Some will embrace the change you seek to create, some

will be skeptical, some will feel threatened by you, and some will oppose change for their own reasons.

So it is important to realize that these people have been conditioned to respond to you in a particular way. They will continue to respond that way until they sense your commitment is for the long haul and trust in their own ability to succeed. The longer you lead like Jesus, the more people will change. As individuals embrace these principles, the work group, family, or community organization will change as well. If your organizational culture does not let you talk freely about Jesus, don't worry. Behave like Jesus. Then when people are attracted to the way you lead and they ask you about it, you are free to share with them your leadership role model. Let people see the leader in your life.

One more tip: don't make the mistake of trying to change other leaders with whom you work. Focus on yourself. Be the change you want to see in others.

Leading like Jesus is lived out minute by minute in big decisions as well as small choices. At some point leading like Jesus will involve going public with your good intentions. That moment could come unexpectedly, perhaps when someone notices something different in the way you are leading and asks you what's going on. Are you prepared to respond?

YOUR PERSONAL LEADERSHIP STATEMENT

Imagine you're standing on a stage in an auditorium filled with the people you live and work with every day. The house lights are up. You can clearly see your spouse, your children and grandchildren, your brothers and sisters, your parents, your friends, your boss, your coworkers, your pastor, and your neighbors.

Take a moment and picture each face looking up at you. All eyes and hearts are opened and focused on you and what you are about to say. You feel the love and anticipation in the air: you can't imagine a more positive, accepting crowd than this one that has gathered to hear you deliver a message of vital importance to you and to them.

But a different feature of the room commands your attention as you begin. On the wall immediately behind the audience is a cross.

Imagine taking a slight step forward, moving even closer to the smiling eyes and faces of these very special people as you begin to speak. You have taken great care in preparing what you are going to say and have written it down to be sure not to forget an important point. You take the folded paper from your pocket and begin to read your own personal statement of intent: you want to lead people like Jesus did. What would you say? Perhaps something like this:

"Thank you all for coming to share this important moment with me. I've invited each of you here because, at one time or another, I have attempted to influence your thinking, behavior, or development. In other words, I have sought to lead each of you somewhere for some purpose, for a good and positive goal. This leadership may have been in a formal way when we were acting out our roles in an organization or informally as part of our life role relationships.

"As a result, we have shared some successes together that left us feeling good about our relationship and about what we accomplished. At other times we shared frustration with both the results and their impact on our relationship. For the times I have led you poorly—out of pride, fear, weariness, or just bad judgment—I apologize and ask for your forgiveness.

"Without dismissing or minimizing the price we all paid for my mistakes, I want today to ask each of you to help me by holding me accountable for leading you at a higher level. I have come to the personal conclusion that to make the most of the influence that has been entrusted to me, I need to follow a trustworthy and relevant leadership role model. I need to model my leadership after someone who will inspire, equip, and walk beside me; someone who calls me to care more about the person than the project; and someone who enables me to bring joy into the places where I lead and the relationships I am blessed with.

"As the old hymn says, 'I have decided to follow Jesus. No turning back, no turning back.' It is my heart's desire—and I am totally committed to following the leadership teachings and example of Jesus in any opportunities I have to influence people's thinking, behavior, and development. I now recognize that, just as Jesus did, I can do this only through an intimate relationship with the Father. I know that my highest purpose in life is to glorify God. I know that loving Him and loving others will give Him glory. As I become more like Jesus, I will lead more like Jesus led. And my leadership will never be about me—it is always about glorifying God—and it's about you, our mission together, and the people we serve.

"Knowing me as you do, you may be thinking this goal sounds impossible—and it sounds that way to me as I hear myself talk. If I were aiming for perfection, that goal would be impossible to attain. If I were promising to deliver uninterrupted progress without relapses, you would be right to dismiss my intentions and put absolutely no hope in seeing those intentions put into practice. But I will start each day asking God—with the guidance of the Holy Spirit—to help me make the best leadership decisions I can. I will ask God to help me glorify Him by serving Jesus Christ and serving you."

PAUSE AND REFLECT

Make this speech your own. What parts will you change and why? When you are pleased with your efforts, will you deliver this speech? You can deliver it with words to an invited audience. You can also deliver it moment by moment through the leadership decisions you make.

In the final section, we will give you the next steps to take and some tools and techniques to adopt that will help you become more and more a Lead Like Jesus leader. It is also our hope that the final section will provide you with ideas for how to refine your skills as well as how to develop new and more effective ways to lead like Jesus.

PART VII

NEXT STEPS TO
LEADING LIKE JESUS

I do not do the good I want to do, but the evil I do not want to do—this I keep on doing. . . . What a wretched man I am! Who will rescue me from this body that is subject to death? Thanks be to God, who delivers me through Jesus Christ our Lord!

Romans 7:19, 24–25

When Paul described himself as a "wretched man," he was essentially saying that he was a work in progress—and aren't we all? Everyone falls short of perfection. It is only in our relationship with the Lord, only through Jesus, that we become more like Him. That transformation is central to leading like Jesus. Only when our transformation is under way can we begin to bring positive change to the lives of the people we touch. In other words, leading like Jesus is about leading change.

Initiating change, modeling change, responding to change, and sustaining long-term change are fundamental aspects of leading. Leadership is about going someplace. It is about bringing the future into view through the acts and choices of today.

When Jesus entered human history as a leader of change, He offered both the means and the model for fulfilling the change He had in mind. His leadership included things that only He could do. The holy work of the cross, for instance, was His alone to complete. Washing the feet of the disciples was a symbol of the work He called all of us to do in His name. In both these works of His hands, Jesus changed the definition of great leadership from a place of power, position, and prestige to the role of humble servant of love.

The change that Jesus came to introduce was not a minor adjustment to current thinking and behavior that would allow for better levels of performance within an existing system. The change He came to lead was radical and revolutionary. He came to turn the world upside down and then right side up by making *love* the preeminent standard for all aspects of relationships. Jesus calls all those who follow Him to carry out their specific assignments in bringing this change to their generation.

No matter what change you are trying to implement, it will not be easy—even when the benefits are overwhelmingly positive. So, in this final section of the book, we will focus on the dynamics of change that have an impact on you, the people around you, and the various organizations in which you participate.

LEADING POSITIVE CHANGE

"Truly I tell you, unless you change and become like little
children, you will never enter the kingdom of heaven."

Matthew 18:3

As we have said, the heart and head of leading like Jesus are internal domains. Thus, great leadership is an inside-out job. It begins with the *heart* question—*Are you here to serve or be served?*—which is reinforced by the Being Habits. Once your heart is right, the Lead Like Jesus journey travels to your *head*, where you develop your beliefs about leading like Jesus. But people won't know what's in your heart and head until you act on it by focusing on having *hands* that lead like Jesus and on cultivating the Doing Habits. But taking what you have learned and actually using it in your daily life as a leader is not easy. Why?

To answer that question, you first have to realize that change happens in all your spheres of influence, from self, to leading another person, to leading others, to leading an organization or a community. Second, you must understand that there are different levels of change and a number of reasons why people resist change.

THE FOUR LEVELS OF CHANGE

Leading lasting change requires understanding and addressing four essential levels of change:[1]

change in knowledge
change in attitude
change in behavior
change in cultural norms and expectations

Let's explore each of these levels of change and see what they require from a leader.

Change in Knowledge

In many respects, change in knowledge is the easiest to accomplish. All you have to do is read or listen to something. In our electronically connected world, access to new information and data is literally at our fingertips.

As Ken's wife, Margie, has often remarked, the gap between not knowing and knowing is a lot smaller than the gap between knowing and doing. Effective change leadership requires providing new information as well as a compelling reason for people to consider changing the way they see the world around them. According to our dear friend Paul J. Meyer, a key component of changing the knowledge base of an individual or a group is "Repetition! Repetition! Repetition!"

A second aspect of effective knowledge transfer is testing for understanding. Leaders who believe that the proclamation of ideas without the verification of understanding equals effective communication are in for a great shock when it comes time for implementation.

As you walk through the Bible and listen to Jesus addressing both crowds and individuals, you'll notice that He continually repeated the same message in a wide variety of formats in order to meet the needs of His audience. He also initiated opportunities for people to ask questions and clarify their understanding. The priority He put on this aspect of leadership is reflected in His prayer to God: "I have revealed you to those whom you gave me out of the world. . . . Now they know that everything you have given me comes from you. For I gave them the words you gave me and they accepted them" (John 17:6–8).

Change in Attitude

Changing attitude is more difficult than changing knowledge because attitude is an emotionally charged bit of knowledge. It's when you feel strongly, in either a positive or a negative way, about something you know. Attitude begins with information, but without context, information is unlikely to generate any enthusiasm for change. So a primary challenge for a change leader is to convince people that what they are being called to do differently is both right and important. For a leader, earning the right to be heard is based on trust. People who trust you will hear what you have to say and, continuing to trust you, probably get on board.

Change in Behavior

Changing behavior is also challenging. It's different from changing knowledge or attitude because now people have to *do* something. For example, the vast majority of smokers will tell you they know smoking is not good for their health. Most also have a positive attitude about the idea of giving up smoking. But to actually stop smoking is not easy, especially if it has been a long-term habit. Ken always kids that he doesn't smoke; he just eats. He knows he is ten to fifteen pounds overweight, and he has a positive attitude about losing those excess pounds, but it is difficult to change his eating behavior—particularly when he is able to smell a piece of cheesecake a mile away. A few years ago, though, something changed. Ken had a compelling vision of the future that involved fulfilling the role God has for him in spreading the Lead Like Jesus message. As a result, today Ken is living a much healthier lifestyle.[2]

If they are to be of any practical use, changes in knowledge and in attitude must inspire changed behavior. At the heart of every New Year's resolution and every promise to be better or do better lies the question of how to put those good intentions into action. Change leaders have to identify behaviors that will move people to the new patterns, model those behaviors, catch people doing things right, and praise progress.

PAUSE AND REFLECT

Think of a personal change you know you should make. You have a positive attitude about doing it, but you haven't taken any steps yet. Why not? Where can you get the help you need to break through this barrier that keeps you from acting?

Change in Cultural Norms and Expectations

This is the most difficult change of all because it involves many people who bring to the party a variety of perceptions about what should or should not be done. As a result, lasting change in community only happens over time, so change leaders have to be in it for the long haul. For change to gain the power needed to transform a culture, each individual must share the basic desire for inclusion and collaboration toward the higher purpose of the community. Consider this powerful example of the beginning of cultural change.

At a Lead Like Jesus training in Ghana, it was no secret that a paramount chief was in the room. Attendees periodically glanced his direction as they shared the astonishing realization that the leader they so respected and feared was listening and learning alongside them.

Ghana's traditional and very powerful leader was introduced to a radical concept that day: servanthood. As is customary at the end of the training program, each participant was given the chance to wash someone's feet. As bucket and rag were passed around the room, everyone followed Jesus' example of leadership and took turns washing the feet of tablemates and neighbors.

Ghanaians' respect for their paramount chief is so great that sometimes it even surpasses their reverence for their president. Subjects must bow, kneel down, or lie prostrate just to speak with their paramount chief. So when the paramount chief of the Ewe Tribe bent down and rested on his knees, it shocked the gathering. He laid aside the headdress that set him apart from his people as he bowed before one of his subordinates. Only Jesus can inspire an action as radically anticultural as a paramount chief kneeling before a subordinate.

Chieftaincy in Ghana is traditionally a religious as well as political institution: customarily, Ghanaians will believe whatever their paramount chief believes. For the paramount chief of the Ewe Tribe to even attend a Lead Like Jesus training meant that the people who were in attendance would pay closer attention to the ideas presented.

After the training, the paramount chief approached a Lead Like Jesus team member. Clearly, the day's teaching had affected him, and only God knew the implications for his tribe and even for his country. "Thank you so much," he said, overcome with emotion. "I love you."

PAUSE AND REFLECT

Think about a time you have been involved—as a leader or as a follower—in a change of cultural norms or expectations. Was it difficult? Why or why not? Did anything in particular help everyone get through the change successfully? If not, what might have helped the transition?

Take heart! Change is difficult, but it will be worth the journey as souls—including yours—are served by God's Spirit and His people.

REASONS WHY LEADING CHANGE IS DIFFICULT

It's been said that the only people who like change are babies with a wet diaper. Why is that so? We have found seven reasons why people resist change.

1. People feel awkward. People naturally want to avoid feeling uncomfortable, but discomfort comes with a change in their way of thinking, their attitude, or their behavior. This awkwardness is perfectly natural. If you don't feel awkward, then you aren't going through change.

   Application: When leading people through change, put

the change in context by explaining what, when, how, and why change is occurring and why it is necessary.

2. **People feel alone.** Even if everyone in the family, the business, or the organization is in the same situation, most of us tend to take it personally when change hits: *Why me?* Fear of having one's personal weaknesses and limitations exposed can result in feelings of isolation and an unwillingness to participate in the change.

When a leader models transparency and provides safe harbors where people can share their concerns, they come to realize they are not alone in their feelings. Experiencing some strength in numbers, they find themselves more open to the change and more confident about it.

Application: During our Lead Like Jesus programs, we conduct EGOs Anonymous meetings where people are encouraged to share how their pride and fears have negatively impacted their lives and relationships. A comment often heard at the end of these sessions is, "I thought I was the only one who felt that way."

3. **People focus on what they have to give up.** People's first reaction to a suggested change is often a personal sense of loss. What do we mean by this? Pride about past achievements, stability in relationships, and a sense of balanced priorities are hard to surrender. So effective leaders of change allow people to honor the past but not live there. These leaders help people acknowledge present realities and reshape their picture of the desired future.

Application: When working with groups undergoing change, we often hold "mourning sessions" where people can talk openly about what they think they will have to give up because of this change. People need a chance to mourn their losses before they can embrace the benefits of the change.

4. **People can handle only so much change.** Change is all around us all the time. To lead a change that will last requires being alert to both the extent and the speed of the change you're asking people to deal with. If the change becomes too much for them to handle, they can become overwhelmed and discouraged despite the positive results you intend. That's why it's best not to change everything all at once. Choose the key areas that will make the biggest difference.

Application: When implementing change, let people experience some success that they can build on before adding more elements. For some, the Ten Commandments seemed to be too many. When He was asked which was the greatest commandment in the Law, Jesus replied: "'Love the Lord your God with all your heart and with all your soul and with all your mind.' This is the first and greatest commandment. And the second is like it: 'Love your neighbor as yourself.' All the Law and the Prophets hang on these two commandments" (Matthew 22:36–40). If people live by these two commandments, they don't necessarily need to remember commandments such as *Thou shall not kill, Thou shall not steal,* or *Thou shall not commit adultery.* In other words, the two greatest commandments Jesus spoke about make everything else clear.

5. **People worry about resources.** Fear of change often expresses itself as the fear of not having enough of what is required to implement the change. This concern can lead to the hoarding of known resources, and then cooperation ends. An effective leader calms people's concern by opening their eyes to the collective resources available.

Application: As the greatest Change Leader of all time, Jesus addressed concerns about resources by pointing His followers to God as the Provider of all they would require:

> "Do not worry, saying, 'What shall we eat?' or 'What shall we drink?' or 'What shall we wear?' For the pagans run after all these things, and your heavenly Father knows that you need them. But seek first his kingdom and his righteousness, and all these things will be given to you as well." (Matthew 6:31–33)

6. **People are at different levels of readiness.** Those who are quickest to raise their hands in support of change may be seeing it through eyes of self-interest. Others, who are slower to be convinced about the value of the change, may make better followers in the long run.

Furthermore, leaders who invest time in clarifying what they have in mind and encouraging those who are initially reluctant can acquire steady allies instead of creating foot-dragging enemies.

Application: The disciples who made up the next generation of leaders—the disciples whom Jesus inspired and equipped to fulfill God's vision—were a varied group of unique personalities and different attitudes toward change. Peter, for instance, represented a highly emotional, quick-to-respond type. The apostle Thomas was slower to accept change, and he required more information before making any commitment. Philip was quick to embrace change, but he wasn't entirely clear about what Jesus had come to do. Jesus dealt with each of these men according to his different needs and personalities. In the end each one followed Him and gave his life in committed service to His vision.

7. **People tend to revert to old behaviors when the pressure to change is removed.** Leading change that will last requires constant reinforcement. It means praising progress, keeping the vision alive, reinforcing the connection between individual effort and organizational success, personally modeling consistent behavior during challenging times, and extending grace and forgiveness to those who lose their way. Each of these aspects of leading effective, long-term change requires the leader to make sacrificial choices. Effective leaders of change must apply constant and consistent pressure until the tipping point is reached and inertia becomes action.

Application: One of the most powerful examples of Jesus reinforcing His vision and values with the disciples, and Peter in particular, is found in John 21:12–19:

> Jesus said to them, "Come and have breakfast." None of the disciples dared ask him, "Who are you?" They knew it was the Lord. Jesus came, took the bread and gave it to them, and did the same with the fish. This was now the third time Jesus appeared to his disciples after he was raised from the dead.
>
> When they had finished eating, Jesus said to Simon Peter, "Simon son of John, do you love me more than these?"
>
> "Yes, Lord," he said, "you know that I love you."
>
> Jesus said, "Feed my lambs."
>
> Again Jesus said, "Simon son of John, do you love me?"
>
> He answered, "Yes, Lord, you know that I love you."
>
> Jesus said, "Take care of my sheep."

The third time he said to him, "Simon son of John, do you love me?"

Peter was hurt because Jesus asked him the third time, "Do you love me?" He said, "Lord, you know all things; you know that I love you."

Jesus said, "Feed my sheep. Very truly I tell you, when you were younger you dressed yourself and went where you wanted; but when you are old you will stretch out your hands, and someone else will dress you and lead you where you do not want to go." Jesus said this to indicate the kind of death by which Peter would glorify God. Then he said to him, "Follow me!"

Leading people through change that will last is difficult. Leaders need to give people a passionate sense of purpose, a compelling vision of the future, and constant reinforcement that the effort will be worthwhile.

PAUSE AND REFLECT

Think about a difficult change that you were called to be involved in as a leader or follower. Reflect on the seven reasons why leading even positive change is hard. What could you have done differently as a leader or follower to make that change effort easier or more successful?

EGOS ANONYMOUS: TAKING THE FIRST STEP TOWARD EXALTING GOD ONLY

The goal of this command is love, which comes from a
pure heart and a good conscience and a sincere faith.

1 Timothy 1:5

As we have said before, we think great leadership is an inside-out
job that starts with your heart. That's where you store your intentions as well as the answer to our often-asked question: "Are you
here to serve or to be served?"

When we ask that question in our sessions, nobody ever raises
his or her hand and says, "I am here to be served." Instead, each
person in attendance wants to be known as someone who is there
for others. Yet we know from the EGOs Anonymous (EA) meetings we hold in our leadership seminars that everyone has to deal,
on a daily basis, with the demons of false pride and fear. In fact,
we believe EGO—Edging God Out—is the biggest addiction of all,
because it motivates every other addiction.

Everyone recognizes that people driven by false pride think more highly of themselves than they should. Yet we contend that people with false pride are often covering up not-okay feelings about themselves and are overcompensating for fear and self-doubt. On the other hand, people who are clearly driven by self-doubt and fear are constantly looking for things outside themselves that will make them feel better about themselves. Sometimes those things are negative addictions such as alcohol, drugs, sex, power, possessions, and the like. So when you don't feel good about yourself, return to the unconditional love of God and the support of His people.

Now back to our EA meetings. We always start by saying, "All EA meetings are voluntary. If your EGO has never gotten in your way through false pride (promoting your self-interest) or through fear (protecting your self-interest), then you can leave." Tens of thousands of people have participated in EA meetings through the years, and no one has ever left.

To give you a sense of how an EGOs Anonymous meeting works, we are going to let you sit in on one as an observer. In a real EA meeting, there are no observers—only people who are actively trying to work on their EGO addiction. The people you will meet are fictitious, but the issues they raise come from real people involved in real-life leadership situations.

WELCOME TO EGOS ANONYMOUS

"Hi. My name is Darnell, and I am an EGOmaniac," said the man standing in front of his folding chair.

"Hi, Darnell," the group replied with a tone of acceptance.

The man continued, "Since our last meeting, my pride affected my leadership at home when it kept me from admitting to myself and to my wife that she was right about a lousy investment choice I had made. Instead of owning my mistake, I got mad at her for being right. It took me too long to apologize." As Darnell sat down, the group applauded, and several of the people in the group nodded in understanding.

Next to stand was a well-dressed businesswoman on the other side of the circle. "My name is Laura," she said in a tone that indicated she was used to speaking in public.

"Hi, Laura," the group responded.

"I am an EGOmaniac," Laura continued. "As the president of a large advertising firm, my pride gets in the way when I become impatient with the people who work for me. Last week, I took back an assignment I had delegated to one of my key new team members and did the work myself. I ended up overloaded, and she ended up demoralized." The usual applause followed as Laura sat back down.

Silence followed, as often happens at an EGOs Anonymous meeting. We may wait several minutes until someone else is ready to share how his or her EGO has sabotaged his or her efforts to be an effective leader. About a minute later, a tall, gray-haired man with a thoughtful face rose slowly. "Hi. My name is Steven," he said in a quiet voice.

The group reached out again: "Hi, Steven."

"I am an EGOmaniac," Steven said. "My EGO takes the form of fear of success. I am the pastor of a rapidly growing church, and I am reluctant to give my approval to plans for further expansion. I am afraid I won't be able to handle any more demands on my time and energy." His humble admission of self-limitation was met with healing applause that signaled understanding.

In sharp contrast to the quiet demeanor of the pastor, the next person to stand was an athletic-looking man in his midthirties whose quick movements and energetic style radiated intensity. "Hi! My name is Tyler."

The group responded, "Hi, Tyler."

"I am an EGOmaniac," Tyler replied. "I coach high school basketball, and my EGO negatively impacts my leadership when my desire to win and my fear of failure cause me to make choices that are not always in the best interest of the growth and development of my players." The group clapped as the openness and honesty of Tyler's statement sank in.

An attractive, casually dressed young woman stood up. "Hi. My name is Darla," she said in a tentative, almost apologetic manner. The group greeted her exactly as they had the other speakers.

"I am an EGOmaniac," Darla continued. "I'm the mother of two small children. My EGO gets in the way when my low self-esteem and fear of inadequacy make me feel like a victim and rob my kids and me of any joy we could be sharing." The group nodded in understanding.

Next, a middle-aged man with a salt-and-pepper beard stood and said, "My name is Rich."

The group encouraged him with their greeting: "Hi, Rich."

"Up until today, I would have said that I was not an EGOmaniac. I really don't have any pride. I know that everything I have comes from God. But today I've discovered that I am an EGOmaniac. I've Edged God Out because of my fear. There are so many things I know He's wanted me to do, and either I haven't attempted them or I've settled for less than what I clearly knew He wanted." The group applauded his confession to demonstrate their support and understanding.

The pattern of reflective silence before and after the sharing of personal triumphs and failures in dealing with false pride and fear continued for another twenty minutes until everyone who wanted to speak had been able to both share and receive encouragement from the group.

PAUSE AND REFLECT

Imagine you were the next person to stand up at this EA meeting. How would you describe the EGO problem that has had the biggest impact on how you lead people?

Admitting you have an EGO problem is the first step of the Lead Like Jesus twelve-step program we have developed for leaders who want to bring new hope and effectiveness into their lives and relationships by leading like Jesus. As you look at the people you influence—those in your organization, your church, and your family—you might feel that constantly leading from a servant's heart and practicing the Doing Habits of grace, forgiveness, encouragement, and community is utterly impossible. If so, remember that this calling to lead isn't about what *we* can do; leading like Jesus is about what God can do through us when we are willing to obey Him and express His love. Because we are empowered and led by God's Holy Spirit, we can wisely and effectively lead others.

In fact, our greatest job as leaders is to let the One who is leading us become visible to others through what we say and do. We felt the best way to do that—and the best way to pull together the beginning steps of the transformation required to lead like Jesus—was to share the full twelve-step program, adapted from Alcoholics Anonymous (AA).[1] The main purpose of EA meetings is to build a community where people can, among other things, encourage one another to accept God's grace and to forgive themselves. Building community is important because true change only happens over time and in community, yet building community requires intimacy and vulnerability. We invite you to join us in a very personal way as we go through the twelve steps of EA.

The Twelve Steps of Lead Like Jesus EGOs Anonymous

1. I admit that on more than one occasion I have allowed my EGO needs and my drive for earthly success to negatively impact my role as a leader. My leadership has not been the servant leadership that Jesus modeled.
2. I've come to believe that God can transform my leadership motives, thoughts, and actions into the servant leadership that Jesus modeled.
3. I've made a decision to turn my leadership efforts over to God and to become a disciple of Jesus and the kind of servant leader He modeled.

These first three steps—admitting you have a problem, realizing that God is the only One who can overcome it, and therefore letting go and letting God—begin your journey to overcoming your EGO issues.

4. I've made a searching and fearless inventory of my own leadership motives, thoughts, and behaviors that are inconsistent with leading like Jesus.
5. I've admitted to God, to myself, and to at least one other person when I've been inconsistent in leading like Jesus in my motives, thinking, and behavior.

These two steps are where you take a hard look at yourself and admit your shortcomings. A few minutes of brutal honesty is worth a year of self-deception.

6. I am entirely ready to have God remove all character defects that keep me from leading like Jesus.
7. I humbly ask God to remove my shortcomings and to strengthen me against the temptations of recognition, power, greed, and fear.

Here is where you come to the realization that God is not your copilot; He is the One flying the plane! Only with Him in charge of your life do you have a chance of overcoming your false pride and fear demons.

8. I've made a list of those people I may have harmed by my EGO-driven leadership, and I am willing to make amends to them all.
9. I've made direct amends to such people whenever possible, unless doing so would injure them or others.
10. I continue to take a regular personal inventory regarding my leadership role, and when I am wrong, I promptly and specifically admit it.

After accepting God's grace and forgiving yourself, your reaching out to those you may have harmed demonstrates to them God's love. This is an ongoing process of accountability; it will be daily work for the rest of your life. The great news is that you never have to walk alone. As they say at the end of most AA meetings, "Keep coming back!"

11. I engage in the disciplines of solitude, prayer, the study of Scripture, and belief in God's unconditional love for me in order to align my leadership with what Jesus modeled and to constantly seek ways to be a servant leader for the people I encounter in my leadership responsibilities.

12. I am committed to carrying the message of leading like Jesus to all those I have an opportunity to influence.

The last two steps are where the Being Habits and the Doing Habits come together: accepting and abiding in God's unconditional love and obeying God and expressing His love. Jesus emphasized the preeminence of God's love when He spelled out the two greatest commandments: "'Love the Lord your God with all your heart and with all your soul and with all your mind and with all your strength' [Being]. The second is this: 'Love your neighbor as yourself' [Doing]. There is no commandment greater than these" (Mark 12:30–31). The best way to fulfill these commandments is to make the twelve EA steps a guide for your life.

While the first step of admitting your addiction is all-important, completing all twelve steps is necessary for you to overcome your addiction to Edging God Out. Give yourself plenty of time to overcome your addiction. And know that if you take this mission seriously, you have a high probability of successfully leading more and more the way Jesus does.

PAUSE AND REFLECT

Remember that completing the twelve steps is a day-by-day journey and an ongoing challenge. The great news is we are not called or designed to travel the journey or face the challenge alone. Listen once again to the promise Jesus makes to all who would follow Him: "Surely I am with you always, to the very end of the age" (Matthew 28:20). That promise is still available to you today.

NEXT STEPS TO LEADING LIKE JESUS: CHECKLIST

Leading like Jesus is not a destination but a journey. Like any good traveler embarking on a journey, you will need to make sure you pack what you need.

Item	√
Personal mission statement that is understandable by a twelve-year-old	
Personal definition of success that mentions God's call and His involvement	
Set of rank-ordered personal operating values to help you decide which road to travel when you find yourself at a crossroads	
Truth tellers who will keep you headed in the right direction	
Journal to record the triumphs, challenges, and lessons learned that you will want to remember and pass along to others	
Well-used instruction manual for daily living	
A commitment to—with God's help—practice the Being Habits: accept and abide in God's love; experience solitude; practice prayer; know and apply Scripture; and maintain supportive relationships	
A commitment to—with God's help—practice the Doing Habits: obey God and express His love, grace, forgiveness, encouragement, and community	
Memorized set of emergency numbers when you are in trouble	
Set of recalibration tools to help keep your path straight	

NEXT STEPS TO LEADING LIKE JESUS: RESOURCE LIST

If you are missing any of the recommended items on your checklist, here are some suggested resources to help you obtain what you need.

Personal Mission Statement

Halftime: Moving from Success to Significance by Bob Buford

Living on Purpose: Finding God's Best for Your Life by Christine and Tom Sine

The Path: Creating Your Mission Statement for Work and for Life by Laurie Beth Jones

The Purpose Driven Life: What on Earth Am I Here For? by Rick Warren

Situational Self Leadership by Ken Blanchard, Laurence Hawkins, and Susan Fowler

Personal Definition of Success That Keeps God in Mind

Breathe: Creating Space for God in a Hectic Life by Keri Wyatt Kent

Experiencing God by Henry T. Blackaby and Claude V. King

Great Attitudes!: 10 Choices for Success in Life by Charles Swindoll

In His Steps by Charles M. Sheldon

It Takes Less Than One Minute to Suit Up for the Lord by Ken Blanchard

Ordering Your Private World by Gordon MacDonald

The Search for Significance: Seeing Your True Worth Through God's Eyes by Robert S. McGee

The Servant Leader: Transforming Your Heart, Head, Hands & Habits by Ken Blanchard and Phil Hodges

The 12 Essentials of Godly Success: Biblical Steps to a Life Well Lived by Tommy Nelson

A Set of Rank-Ordered Personal Operating Values

The Heart of Business by Matt Hayes and Jeff Stevens

Managing by Values: How to Put Your Values into Action for Extraordinary Results by Ken Blanchard and Michael O'Connor

The Power of Ethical Management by Ken Blanchard and Norman Vincent Peale

Spiritual Leadership: Moving People on to God's Agenda by Henry T. Blackaby and Richard Blackaby

Transforming Leadership: Jesus' Way of Creating Vision, Shaping Values and Empowering Change by Leighton Ford

Truth Tellers to Keep You Headed in the Right Direction

As Iron Sharpens Iron: Building Character in a Mentoring Relationship by Howard Hendricks and William Hendricks

Brothers! Calling Men into Vital Relationships by Geoff Gorsuch with Dan Schaffer

The Heart of Mentoring: Ten Proven Principles for Developing People to Their Fullest Potential by David Stoddard with Robert J. Tamasy

Woman to Woman: Preparing Yourself to Mentor by Edna Ellison and Tricia Scribner

Women Mentoring Women: Ways to Start, Maintain, and

Expand a Biblical Women's Ministry by Vickie Kraft and
Gwynne Johnson

Well-Used Instruction Manuals for Daily Living

Lead Like Jesus devotions (Visit www.leadlikejesus.com to
sign up.)

Let Go by Francois Fenelon

Life of the Beloved: Spiritual Living in a Secular World by Henri
Nouwen

Living Beyond the Daily Grind by Charles Swindoll

My Utmost for His Highest by Oswald Chambers

NIV Leadership Bible: Leading by the Book (Zondervan)

One Solitary Life by James A. Francis and Ken Blanchard

The Prayer of Jabez: Breaking Through to the Blessed Life by
Bruce Wilkinson

*Small Changes for a Better Life: Daily Steps to Living God's Plan
for You* by Elizabeth George

Streams in the Desert by L. B. Cowman

Practice the Being Habits

- Accept and Abide in God's Love
- Experience Solitude
- Practice Prayer
- Know and Apply Scripture
- Maintain Supportive Relationships

Practice the Doing Habits

- Obey God and Express His Love
- Grace
- Forgiveness
- Encouragement
- Community

A Memorized Set of Emergency Numbers to Call When You Are in Trouble

Thought Conditioners: Forty Powerful Spiritual Phrases That Can Change the Quality of Your Life by Norman Vincent Peale and C. S. Moore

Philippians 4:6–7	Fear
Psalm 23	Fear
Psalm 55:22	Anxiety
Matthew 6:25	Worry
1 Corinthians 10:13	Temptation
Romans 12:3	Pride
Proverbs 13:10	Pride
Jeremiah 9:23–24	Values
1 John 1:9	Repentance
Proverbs 3:5–6	Guidance
Psalm 143:10	Guidance

A Recalibration Tool to Help Keep Your Path Straight

Chapter 32 of this book: "EGOs Anonymous: Taking the First Step Toward Exalting God Only"

DISCUSSION GUIDE

To help enrich your understanding and enable your application of the leadership principles discussed in this book, we have prepared a summary of key concepts contained in *Lead Like Jesus Revisited*. Each key concept is followed by one or more discussion questions. In addition to reviewing the key lessons in each section, this interactive guide will stimulate thought and conversation about how to apply these concepts to each participant's own leadership style.

We encourage you to proceed through the discussion guide at your own pace. It is useful for individual study, but it is designed primarily for use in a group setting—which we highly recommend—after everyone in the group has read the book. We hope by reading *Lead Like Jesus Revisited* and sharing this learning experience with others that you will not only acquire a deeper understanding of what leading like Jesus is all about but also be inspired to incorporate the principles into your daily leadership opportunities.

Before you get into your discussions, picture yourself and your Lead Like Jesus group going on a relaxing walk with Jesus. You feel loved and secure, free to stop along the way to ask questions and listen carefully to the Lord's answers. Listen, too, as He calls your name and says to you once more: "Come to me, all you who are weary and burdened, and I will give you rest. Take my yoke upon you and learn from me, for I am gentle and humble in heart, and you will find rest for your souls. For my yoke is easy and my burden is light" (Matthew 11:28–30).

Blessings to you as you continue your journey.

PART I: A BIBLICAL PERSPECTIVE ON LEADERSHIP (PAGES 1–38)

The formula *Everything – Love = Nothing* is not of our making. It is the irrefutable law of the kingdom of God, perfectly fulfilled by Jesus. It is also the defining characteristic of the leadership model of Jesus: leading like Jesus means loving like Jesus.

Key Concept 1

Leadership is an influence process. Anytime you seek to influence the thinking, behavior, or development of someone in your personal or professional life, you are taking on the role of a leader.

1. Think of two situations in which you currently act in a leadership role: one as an organizational leader and one in a life role leadership situation. In what ways are these leadership roles different from each other? In what ways are these roles alike?
2. What basic question do you have to ask yourself and answer honestly if you are going to seek to lead like Jesus in both situations?
3. What about each of these leadership roles makes it difficult for you to follow through on seeking to serve rather than to be served?

Key Concept 2

"Jesus called [his disciples] together and said, 'You know that the rulers of the Gentiles lord it over them, and their high officials exercise authority over them. *Not so with you.* Instead, whoever wants to become great among you must be your servant, and whoever wants to be first must be your slave—just as the Son of Man did not come to be served, but to serve, and to give his life as a ransom for many'" (Matthew 20:25–28).

1. Jesus called His followers to an approach to leadership that was radically different from what they saw in the world around them. As a modern-day follower of Jesus, describe the general pattern of leadership you have observed and experienced in today's society.
2. Is the leadership Jesus expected from His followers any more or any less radical today than it was in the first century? Explain your answer.
3. Given the complexity and potential impact of leadership decisions in a global economy, what modifications do you think Jesus would make in His instructions to modern leaders?
4. Name three specific ways Jesus would approach your leadership responsibilities differently than you approach them.

Key Concept 3

Learning to lead like Jesus is a transformational journey (illustrated in the spheres of influence diagram on page 24) that begins with self-examination. Then you move on to leading another person in a one-on-one relationship, then to leading others, and finally to leading an organization or community.

1. Whose are you? Who are you? What impact can knowing the answers to those questions have on your leadership?
2. Name three ways you nurture trust in your one-on-one relationships at work and at home.
3. Discuss a time when you lost trust in a leader and the impact that experience had on your relationship.
4. What words would people in your family use to describe your leadership in the following situations:
   - a time of crisis
   - a time of failure
   - a time of victory
   - a time of plenty
   - a time of want
5. What is most likely to occur when leaders try to drive change at the organizational level without first addressing the issue of their own credibility at the personal, one-on-one, and team leadership levels?

Key Concept 4

Leading like Jesus involves the alignment of four leadership domains: *heart*, *head*, *hands*, and *habits*. The internal domains— the motivation of your *heart* and the leadership perspective of your *head*—are hidden or even disguised if it suits your purpose. The external domains—your *hands*, or your public leadership behavior, and your *habits* as experienced by others—influence greatly whether people will follow you.

1. Briefly describe in your own words what is meant by the terms *heart*, *head*, *hands*, and *habits* of leadership.
2. What thought from this section was most striking, convicting, or significant? How will you implement it? By when?

PART II: THE HEART OF A GREAT LEADER (PAGES 39–83)

A changed heart means a changed leader.

Key Concept 1

What does your heart have to do with leadership? *Everything*! In the heart is our *why*.

1. Have you ever experienced a challenge so big that you had to go back to the core of what you believed about God and review the basics? Those beliefs are stored in your heart, and they shape you and every relationship in your life.

   Answer these fundamental questions:
   - Is God good?
   - Do you believe He has a plan and purpose for your life?
   - Do you believe anyone or anything can change God's plan for you?
   - Do you believe God loves you?
   - Do you believe God will use everything in your life for His glory and your good as He promised?
   - Can you trust Him with all of the details of your life?
2. The core of leading like Jesus is love. In which of your relationships do you find it a challenge to lead and love like Jesus?
3. What one step will you take today to strengthen one of those relationships?

Key Concept 2

If you want to follow the mandate Jesus gave us—to serve rather than be served—know that every day your good intentions will be challenged. Our adversary consistently tries to get us to serve ourselves. To better resist that temptation to be drawn off course, we must understand the dynamics of our self-serving EGO that Edges God Out.

1. List three things other than God that people worship and look to for either security or a sense of identity. Why do we human beings trust these things even though we know they are neither stable nor trustworthy?

2. Invite God to guide your thinking about the last time pride got in the way of your leadership. Briefly describe the circumstances. What triggered your pride? When you realized you wanted a do-over, how did you feel? What was the reaction of others to your handling of the situation? What was the result of your mishandling the situation? Do you need to apologize to anyone? What has God shown you—and what does He want you to do?

3. When you face a difficult and uncomfortable decision, which of the following fears are most likely to prevent you from following through on your good intentions and instead prompt a "fight or flight" response?

- fear of rejection
- fear of inadequacy
- fear of death
- fear of success
- fear of loneliness
- fear of loss of control
- fear of losing
- fear of humiliation
- fear of public speaking
- fear of failure
- fear of intimacy
- fear of the future
- fear of want
- fear of pain
- fear of ridicule
- fear of conflict
- fear of tests

What truth from God's Word speaks to these fears? Write the Scripture references here and a helpful verse on an index card you can carry with you or put on the dashboard of your car.

4. Describe a time when emotions overpowered reason and you acted according to your fears rather than your good intentions. What was the result?

5. Listen for the I factor in your conversations. Note your words and your thoughts that reveal *less than* (fearful) or *more than* (prideful) thinking. Also notice how often you turn a conversation back to yourself or interrupt someone's story to tell your own. Are your conversations laced with *I, my,* or *me*? And what do your observations and answers tell you about yourself: Are you more others-focused or more self-focused? If the latter, could you be on the path to Edging God Out?

Key Concept 3

A life intentionally lived with a focus on Jesus and a deep commitment to Him will help you move from Edging God Out to Exalting God Only.

1. Imagine your pride and fear being replaced by genuine humility and confidence grounded in God. What impact would that exchange have in your leadership roles and in your relationships?

2. What about your current concept of God might be keeping you from receiving His unconditional love and accepting His promises as the source of your security and self-worth?

3. Imagine you are sitting down with Jesus today just before He sends you off to represent His kingdom where you work and

in all your personal relationships. Answer these questions
Jesus might ask.

- Do you love Me?
- Do you trust Me?
- Will you serve Me by serving others?
- Do you believe I will always love you regardless of your performance or other people's opinions?
- Are you willing to set aside recognition, power, and instant gratification to honor Me by doing the right thing?
    The more times you answered yes, the more ready you are.

4. What thought from this section did you find most significant? What will you do to implement it in your life—and by when will you do so?

PART III: THE BEING HABITS (PAGES 85–122)

Adopting the Being Habits is essential for those who choose Jesus as their role model for leadership. He led with five key Being Habits—and if we want to lead like Jesus, we will too.

Key Concept 1

Accepting and abiding in God's love requires the foundational belief that His love for you is possible. Believing that it is possible for God to love you will lead you to Him—and He enables us to believe He loves us by His Son's death on the cross and His Holy Spirit's work in our hearts.

1. Think of a time when you felt loved by God. What were the circumstances? What steps could you take to feel His

love now? One step is simply to ask your heavenly Father to reveal His love to you.

Key Concept 2

Solitude is by far the most elusive habit in our modern world of noise, busyness, and 24/7 communications. Solitude is truly countercultural and therefore a challenging behavior to adopt.

1. When did you last spend a significant amount of time with God in solitude—and that means without a to-do or prayer list? When was the last time you sat quietly in God's presence, listening for His still small voice?
2. What keeps you from being alone with God more often? What are the biggest barriers to such solitude that you face—and what has worked for you, enabling you to overcome them?

Key Concept 3

Prayer is an essential act of the will that demonstrates whether we are really serious about living and leading like Jesus. Without prayer, we will never be able to connect our plans and leadership efforts to God's plan for His kingdom.

1. Describe your prayer life in terms of when, what, where, how, and why. What are the richest aspects of prayer for you? Which aspects of your prayer life need improvement?
2. You probably pray *about* people and situations, and that's important. But imagine that the next time you face an important challenge or temptation, you first pray *for* the people involved. What impact might that have on how you approach and interact with those people?

3. What is your prayer strategy for each person, situation, and leadership opportunity in your life? If you don't have one, create one now. Maybe start with some of the when, what, where, how, and why questions. Also, to whom can you go for counsel about a prayer strategy and a strong prayer life?

Key Concept 4

In *Scripture* you discover that God loves you, He has great plans for you, and He created you perfectly to accomplish a specific purpose. Scripture also teaches us how to treat one another, how to love as we have been loved, and how to lead like Jesus.

1. Describe a time when you faced a decision and your knowledge of Scripture made a difference in your choice. What was the result?
2. Are you actively seeking God's guidance by spending time reading, studying, and meditating on Scripture? What is He currently saying to you?
3. Share your favorite verse with your group and talk about why it is your favorite.

Key Concept 5

Leadership can be a lonely business filled with great amounts of soul-draining human interaction but little soul-filling intimacy. Without some *safe-harbor relationships* where we leaders can relax in confidential and unguarded conversation, we become vulnerable to two debilitating frames of mind and spirit: the victim and the martyr.

1. Name the special people in your life who love you enough to tell you what you need to hear. What are you doing to strengthen these special relationships? What people in your

life need you to hold them accountable? Do you love them enough to tell them what they need to know?

2. List three things you do to make it easy for your truth tellers to help you—and then list three things you do that make it difficult for your truth tellers to tell you what you probably don't want to hear.

3. Who in your life is looking to you to be their truth teller? What do you understand that role to look like? Be specific. Describe your partnership with Jesus in this role.

4. What thought from this section did you find most significant? What will you do to implement it in your life— and what deadline will you set for yourself?

PART IV: THE HEAD OF A GREAT LEADER (PAGES 123–64)

When we realize that God is our primary authority and audience and that we are here to please Him alone, our good intentions travel to our *heads*.

Key Concept 1

Your compelling vision will be important in guiding and aligning the efforts of those who are to follow you, or their whole relationship with you is built on a false foundation of who you are.

1. If you are successful in your life purpose and relationships, what would your ideal future look like? Be specific.

2. Imagine your ten-year-old daughter asking you, "What are the four most important values in our family?" What are they?

3. Remember that assessing your life purpose, your picture of the future, your values, and your goals is an ongoing process. In what specific way(s) can your compelling vision be used for your greater good and the greater good of those you lead? And what can you do to glorify God as you seek to fulfill that vision?

Key Concept 2

Jesus stayed focused on what He was sent to accomplish during His season of leadership on earth. In total obedience and commitment, Jesus stayed on task. He did not seek to take on other projects or the agenda others hoped He would fulfill.

1. As a leader, list three things that are most likely to pull you off course from your purpose. What impact would your changing course or direction have on the morale of the people you lead?
2. Think of a time in your life when a leader stayed strong and on task despite tremendous pressure to give up or give in. What was the long-range impact on your desire to follow and trust that leader?

Key Concept 3

People skeptical about our approach to great leadership contend that the words *servant* and *leader* don't go together. How can a person both lead *and* serve? People who think that way don't understand the two parts to the great leadership Jesus exemplified: The visionary role—setting the course and the destination—is the *leadership* aspect of great leadership. The implementation role—doing things the right way with a focus on serving—is the *servant* aspect of great leadership.

1. Describe in your own words the two parts of leadership—vision and implementation—and the role of the leader in

creating an environment where people get excited about both where they are headed and how they are going to get there.

2. Think for a moment about how well you serve those around you. What do you do to help those you lead live according to the organization's vision? What do you do to help family members live according to the family's vision? Leadership is not about power. Leadership is not about control. It's about helping people live according to the organization's or family's vision and, ultimately, God's vision.

3. What thought from this section did you find most significant? What will you do to implement it in your life— and what deadline will you set for yourself?

PART V: THE HANDS OF A GREAT LEADER (PAGES 165–208)

Hands provide a powerful symbol of the *doing* aspect of leading like Jesus. With His hands, Jesus rescued the fearful, reassured the doubting, restored the fallen, and beckoned the already occupied to a higher calling and a special personal relationship with Him.

Key Concept 1

Jesus was the preeminent performance coach, and He changed His leadership style appropriately as His disciples developed individually and as a group. Jesus also empowered His followers to carry on the work of sharing the salvation message after He was gone. Through His *hands*—through His effectiveness as a servant leader—Jesus was able to communicate to His disciples what was in His *heart* and His *head* about servant leadership.

1. Describe a time when you were involved in a failure of communication that resulted in a vast difference between what was expected and what was delivered. Recall the frustration and wasted energy that could have been avoided by initially testing for understanding.
2. Only with day-to-day coaching can a leader ensure that the dual goals of positive results and healthy relationships will be reached. List three things that happen when a leader delegates responsibility but fails to provide help and guidance along the way.

Key Concept 2

For individuals to advance from novice to master/teacher, they need leadership partners who can give them whatever direction and support they need to progress to the next stage of learning.

1. Describe a time when you were an untrained novice facing a new task or role. In order to get started, what did you need most from someone? Did you get what you needed? If not, what was the result?
2. Describe a time when you were learning something new and needed someone to push you beyond a failure or an easy early success so that you could get to a higher level of understanding and performance. Think of a time when you quit because nobody was around to help you step up to the next level. What are you doing as a leader to determine who among those you lead needs to be helped or pushed? What signs of being ready to quit do you watch for?
3. Can you remember a time when you felt underappreciated for a job well done? What if your leader had come alongside

you with some small sign of appreciation? What effect would that kindness have had on you?

4. Describe a time when you were given the opportunity to teach and guide others in what you yourself had recently learned. In what ways did your being prepared as a follower affect how you led others?

Key Concept 3

The true test of great leadership comes when the EGO of the leader and the EGO of the follower engage one another. How well they recognize and overcome the pride and fear in their relationship will determine whether they move toward the mutual satisfaction of commonly held goals—or share in frustrations of their own making.

1. The ideal relationship between a leader and a follower is characterized by mutual service and trust. Describe a time when you, as either a leader or a follower, experienced this type of working relationship. What behaviors helped produce this positive experience and effective partnership?

2. In what ways do you help your people become high performers? Be specific. What can you do to make your relationship with your people a true partnership? Identify the first step you want to take and decide when you will implement it.

3. What thought from this section did you find most significant? What will you do to implement it in your life—and what deadline will you set for yourself?

PART VI: THE DOING HABITS
(PAGES 209–43)

We will not lead differently until we become different people through the transformation that results from our relationship with Jesus. We can't lead like Jesus without following Jesus.

Key Concept 1

Grace is believing that people are doing the best they can, given their level of awareness. It is up to us to make sure grace is extended; we lead in the way of grace.

1. Describe in your own words what it means for you as a leader to extend grace to someone under your authority or in your circle of influence.
2. Who in your family or workplace especially needs grace right now? Go now to be an agent of grace.

Key Concept 2

Out of the depth of your relationship with God, you can seek to be willing to forgive. It is in this place of being willing to forgive that you can find the ability to extend forgiveness to another.

1. Why is extending forgiveness an important aspect of leadership?
2. What price must be paid if true forgiveness is to have a positive impact on the future of a relationship?
3. Whom do you need to forgive in order to restore a productive relationship with this person who let you down?

Key Concept 3

Encouragement changes our perspectives in a moment. Jesus modeled encouragement during His season of leadership.

1. What are some phrases you wish you had heard more often when you were growing up? Spread some of those phrases to at least three people today—and don't forget your family.
2. List the names of some people who need an encouraging word or act from you. What specifically does each one need? When can you give it?

Key Concept 4

Living in community was God's idea, and He has given us instructions for how best to build community.

1. Do you have an accountability group? If not, think of ways you could strengthen your relationships with others by participating in this kind of Christian fellowship.

Key Concept 5

Foundational to leading like Jesus is embracing a life purpose of loving God and loving and serving people.

1. In 1 Corinthians 13 the apostle Paul wrote that love is patient, kind, generous, courteous, humble, unselfish, good tempered, guileless, and sincere. Ask yourself these questions about each trait of love:
   - When does my life reflect this aspect of love?
   - When do I especially struggle to live out this aspect of love?
2. Think of a time when doing the loving thing instead of the popular thing, the easiest thing, or the safest thing would

have restored or retained trust. What kept you from doing the loving thing? Remember this experience for future reference.

Key Concept 6

From a practical point of view, leading like Jesus accomplishes the dual objective of great leadership—results and relationships.

1. When your current season of influence ends, which of the following do you want to be your legacy? Why?
   - Improved service to your customers
   - Enhanced development of the talents and gifts of the people under your influence
   - Made a significant impact on the world around you
2. List two action steps toward the goal you chose that you will commit to taking in the next thirty days.
3. What thought from this section did you find most significant? What will you do to implement it in your life—and what deadline will you set for yourself?

PART VII: NEXT STEPS TO LEADING LIKE JESUS (PAGES 245–67)

Key Concept 1

Taking what you have learned about leading like Jesus and applying it in your daily life as a leader is not easy. One reason is that most people naturally resist change. That's why leading people through change requires a passionate sense of purpose, a compelling vision of the future, and constant reinforcement that the effort will be worthwhile.

1. Think about a change you were called to be involved in as a leader or a follower that was difficult for you. Reflect on the seven reasons why leading even positive change is hard (see pages 252–57). What could you have done differently as a leader or a follower to make that change easier and/or more successful?

Key Concept 2

We all want to be known as someone who is there for others, yet we know that everyone has to deal, on a daily basis, with the demons of false pride and fear. We need to be sure our EGO is Exalting God Only and not Edging God Out.

1. Think for a minute and come up with one instance at work and one outside of work where your EGO was an obstacle to your being an effective leader. What can you do to overcome pride and fear when you become aware that they are affecting your decisions or your performance as a leader?

Key Concept 3

Leading like Jesus is a one-step-at-a-time journey and day-by-day challenge, not a final destination. And leading like Jesus can be done only in the power of the Holy Spirit and with committed, supportive relationships, first with God and then with others. Staying the course in this journey means frequently checking where you are and where you are headed and making any necessary course corrections.

1. For each of the four leadership domains, list one action item you feel would be the hardest for you to continually improve *without the help of the Holy Spirit.*

Heart:

Head:

Hands:

Habits:

Key Concept 4

One unique resource for followers of Jesus is the active presence of the Holy Spirit as Counselor and Guide in our lives. Jesus promised in John 14:26, "The Advocate, the Holy Spirit, whom the Father will send in my name, will teach you all things and will remind you of everything I have said to you."

1. Using your own words, write out a prayer to God. Invite the Holy Spirit to take control of your heart, head, hands, and habits as you seek to gain victory over obstacles that stand in the way of your leading like Jesus. Repeat this process often—for the rest of your life. God bless.

ACKNOWLEDGMENTS

From Ken: I'm thankful for my wife, Margie; our son, Scott; his wife, Madeleine; our daughter, Debbie; and all of our grandchildren for bringing a continuous stream of joy into my life. I'm also grateful for my administrative and editorial support team, Margery Allen, Martha Lawrence, Renee Broadwell, and Anna Espino, for keeping me in line and making me smile.

From Phil: Thank you to my wife, Jane, for her loving support, candor, and patience; to Philip and Marion Hodges and Paul and LeeAnne Pinner for their inspiration as the loving parents of our seven grandchildren; and to my sister, Liz Pavoni, for her constant encouragement.

From Phyllis: Thank you to my family for their constant support, unconditional love, and encouragement in every season of my life and particularly as I have been writing *Lead Like Jesus Revisited*. You remind me of what leading like Jesus looks like in real life, and your lives push me to teach others about the daily difference Jesus makes. Thank you to Jesus—the one who inspires me moment to moment to grow His dream in me to become more like Him and teach others to do the same.

From the authors: Besides our three-member Consultant Team of the Father, the Son, and the Holy Spirit, the authors want to acknowledge the contributions of the following servant leaders:

- Karen McGuire, for continuing to lovingly proofread and edit for the Lead Like Jesus ministry. Karen's contribution to *Lead*

Like Jesus and now to *Lead Like Jesus Revisited* has been critical in capturing the Lead Like Jesus message. Karen's heart for Jesus, her heart to serve, and her heart for excellence shine through on every page.

- Renee Broadwell, for her patience and great skill in editing our final work to ensure the message of this book was the message we meant it to be.
- Avery Willis and Lee Ross, our coauthors of the *Lead Like Jesus: Beginning the Journey* study guide, for the many concepts we developed together.
- The Lead Like Jesus team, who continue to demonstrate leading like Jesus in everyday tasks both great and small.
- Jack Countryman, who believed in the Lead Like Jesus message early on.
- Dallas Willard, for his high scholarship and wisdom in calling us into a deeper and more intimate relationship with Jesus.
- Henry Blackaby, for his unwavering focus on abiding in the heart, mind, and will of God.
- Robert S. McGee, for his concept of Satan's formula for self-worth being the sum of your performance plus the opinion of others.
- Bill Hybels, our coauthor on *Leadership by the Book,* who inspired our journey to study the heart, head, hands, and habits of leading like Jesus.

NOTES

Chapter 2: The Greatest Leadership Role Model of All Time

1. Ken Blanchard first developed Situational Leadership® with Paul Hersey in the late 1960s. It was in the early 1980s that Blanchard and the founding associates of the Ken Blanchard Companies— Margie Blanchard, Don Carew, Eunice Parisi-Carew, Fred Finch, Calla Crafts, Laurie Hawkins, Pat Zigarmi, and Drea Zigarmi— created a new generation of the theory, called Situational Leadership® II. The best description of this thinking can be found in Kenneth Blanchard, Patricia Zigarmi, and Drea Zigarmi, *Leadership and the One Minute Manager* (New York: William Morrow, 1985).

Chapter 4: Is Jesus a Relevant Role Model for Us Today?

1. William Barclay, "Commentary on John 14:1," *The New Daily Study Bible*, http://www.studylight.org/commentaries/dsb/view.cgi?bk=42 &ch=14&vs=1.

Chapter 6: The Four Domains of Leading Like Jesus

1. John Ortberg, *The Life You've Always Wanted: Spiritual Disciplines for Ordinary People* (1997; repr., Grand Rapids: Zondervan, 2002), 167.

Part II: The Heart of a Great Leader

1. A. W. Tozer, *The Knowledge of the Holy: The Attributes of God: Their Meaning in the Christian Life*, 1st gift ed. (New York: HarperSanFrancisco, 1992), 1.

Chapter 8: I Want to Lead Like Jesus, But My Heart Does Not

1. Robert S. McGee, *The Search for Significance: Your True Worth Through God's Eyes* (Nashville: W Publishing, 2003), 21.

Chapter 9: The Results of a Heart Out of Order

1. Inspired by C. S. Lewis, *The Screwtape Letters* (repr., New York: HarperCollins, 2001), 44: "an ever-increasing craving for an ever-diminishing pleasure."

Chapter 10: Warning Signs on the Path to Edging God Out

1. Francis Fisher Browne, *The Every-day Life of Abraham Lincoln: A Narrative and Descriptive Biography with Pen-Pictures and Personal Recollections by Those Who Knew Him* (Chicago: Browne & Howell, 1914), 408–10.
2. Leighton Ford, *Transforming Leadership: Jesus' Way of Creating Vision, Shaping Values and Empowering Change* (Downers Grove, IL: InterVarsity Press, 1991), 261.
3. Gordon MacDonald, *Ordering Your Private World* (Wheaton, IL: Tyndale, 2003).

Chapter 11: A Heart Turnaround

1. Jim Collins, *Good to Great: Why Some Companies Make the Leap . . . and Others Don't* (New York: HarperCollins, 2001), 35.
2. Ken Blanchard and Norman Vincent Peale, *The Power of Ethical Management* (New York: William Morrow, 1988), 39.
3. Fred Smith, *Breakfast with Fred* (Ventura, CA: Regal Books/Gospel Light, 2007), 166.

Part III: The Being Habits

1. Rick Warren, *The Purpose Driven Life: What on Earth Am I Here For?* (Grand Rapids: Zondervan, 2002), 175.

Chapter 14: The Habit of Practicing Prayer

1. Oswald Chambers, *My Utmost for His Highest* (New York: Dodd, Mead, 1935), 171.
2. Johnson Oatman Jr., "Count Your Blessings," 1897.

Chapter 16: The Habit of Maintaining Supportive Relationships

1. Ken Blanchard and Colleen Barrett, *Lead with LUV: A Different Way to Create Real Success* (Upper Saddle River, NJ: Financial Times Press, 2011), 106.

2. Ken Blanchard, Bill Hybels, and Phil Hodges, *Leadership by the Book: Tools to Transform Your Workplace* (New York: William Morrow, 1999), 110.

Part IV: The Head of a Great Leader

1. Ken Blanchard and Jesse Lyn Stoner, *Full Steam Ahead! Unleash the Power of Vision in Your Work and Your Life* (San Francisco: Berrett-Koehler, 2003), 79.

Chapter 17: Developing Your Own Compelling Vision

1. Susan Fowler developed this process for the Situational Self Leadership program offered by the Ken Blanchard Companies. For more information, see www.kenblanchard.com.
2. Ken Blanchard and Michael O'Connor, *Managing by Values: How to Put Your Values into Action for Extraordinary Results* (San Francisco: Berrett-Koehler, 1997), 112.

Chapter 19: Creating a Compelling Team/Organizational Vision

1. Lewis Carroll, *Alice's Adventures in Wonderland and Through the Looking Glass* (1865/1872; repr., New York: Cosimo Books, 2010), 41.
2. Everything written here about Louisiana State Penitentiary, Warden Burl Cain, and the Malachi Dads program came from visits by Phyllis Hendry and Phil Hodges to the prison and in-person discussions with Warden Cain.
3. Pew Charitable Trusts, *Collateral Costs: Incarceration's Effects on Economic Mobility* (Washington, DC: Pew Charitable Trusts, 2010), 18; Roger Weeder, "Breaking the Cycle: Children Who Have Parents in Jail," Operation New Hope, May 6, 2015, http://operationnewhope.org/breaking-the-cycle-children-who-have-parents-in-jail/.
4. Jeff James, "Standards with Purpose," *Talking Point: The Disney Institute Blog*, September 4, 2012, https://disneyinstitute.com/blog/2012/09/standards-with-purpose/94/.
5. Ken first heard this concept of great leaders being like third-grade teachers from Max DePree, the legendary former chairman of Herman Miller.
6. Ken Blanchard, John P. Carlos, and Alan Randolph, *Empowerment Takes More Than a Minute* (San Francisco: Berrett-Koehler, 1996).

Chapter 20: Implementing Your Compelling Vision

1. Bob Buford, *Halftime: Moving from Success to Significance* (Grand Rapids: Zondervan, 1994), 197.

Chapter 22: The Work of the Carpenter

1. Henry Drummond, *The Greatest Thing in the World* (Chicago: Revell, 1891), 32.

Chapter 23: The Way of the Carpenter

1. John MacArthur, *Twelve Ordinary Men: How the Master Shaped His Disciples for Greatness—and What He Wants to Do with You* (Nashville: Thomas Nelson, 2002).
2. Ibid., 39.
3. More than forty years ago, Ken began developing Situational Leadership® with Paul Hersey. Today, the latest version of that concept, called Situational Leadership® II, is used widely around the world to help leaders develop high-performing leader-follower relationships. It was not until the late 1980s, when Ken became a believer and read the Bible, that he realized how compatible the concepts contained in Situational Leadership® II were with the biblical record of how Jesus trained and developed His disciples as He moved them from call to commission. In fact, this Way of the Carpenter model is an adaptation of the Situational Leadership® II model. To find out more about Situational Leadership® II, read Ken Blanchard, Patricia Zigarmi, and Drea Zigarmi, *Leadership and the One Minute Manager: Increasing Effectiveness Through Situational Leadership* (New York: Harper Collins, 1985).

Chapter 25: The Habit of Obeying God and Expressing His Unconditional Love

1. Henry Drummond, *The Greatest Thing in the World* (Chicago: Revell, 1891), 18.

Chapter 29: The Habit of Community

1. Rod Handley, *Character Counts: Who's Counting Yours?* (Grand Island, NE: Cross Training, 2002), 35–36.

Chapter 31: Leading Positive Change

1. Ken Blanchard et al., *Leading at a Higher Level* (Upper Saddle River, NJ: Financial Times Press, 2009), 215.

2. If you are interested in learning more about Ken's journey to a healthier lifestyle, read *Fit at Last* (San Francisco: Berrett-Koehler, 2014), which Ken Blanchard coauthored with his fitness coach, Tim Kearin.

Chapter 32: EGOs Anonymous: Taking the First Step Toward Exalting God Only

1. Alcoholics Anonymous, *The Big Book of Alcoholics Anonymous* (New York: Works Publishing, 1939).

ABOUT THE AUTHORS

KEN BLANCHARD

Ken Blanchard is one of the most influential leadership experts in the world. A prominent speaker and author, he has coauthored more than sixty books, including *The New One Minute Manager*®. His books have combined sales of more than 21 million copies in forty-two languages. Ken and his wife, Margie, cofounded the Ken Blanchard Companies®, a leading international training and consulting firm.

Ken had been teaching effective leadership principles for years when he began to study the Bible. He soon became fascinated with how Jesus led perfectly in every way, transforming twelve ordinary, unlikely individuals into the first generation of Christian leaders and launching a movement that continues to affect the course of world history more than two thousand years later.

Inspired by Jesus' model of leadership, Ken and his lifelong friend Phil Hodges cofounded the Lead Like Jesus global ministry.

PHIL HODGES

Phil Hodges served as a human resources and industrial relations manager for Xerox Corporation and U.S. Steel for thirty-six years. In 1997 he became a consulting partner with the Ken Blanchard Companies®, where he focused on issues relating to leadership and customer service. In 1999 Phil cofounded the Lead Like Jesus leadership ministry with friend Ken Blanchard.

In addition to helping men and women of faith walk their talk in the marketplace, Phil has a passion for bringing effective leadership principles into the church. Acting on that passion, he served as member and chairman of his local church elder council for more than ten years.

Phil is coauthor of five books, including two he wrote with his friend Ken Blanchard: *Lead Like Jesus: Lessons from the Greatest Leadership Role Model of All Time* and *Lead Like Jesus for Churches*.

Phil finds great joy in living out his life role relationships of husband, father, and grandpa. He and his wife, Jane Kinnaird Hodges, live in Southern California.

PHYLLIS HENDRY

Phyllis Hendry is president and CEO of the Lead Like Jesus global ministry. She is also a sought-after keynote speaker who travels throughout the United States and the world to deliver hope-filled messages straight from her heart, sharing the stage with such notables as Ken Blanchard, John Ortberg, Patrick Lencioni, and Henry Blackaby. Phyllis also enjoys speaking in such intimate settings as church congregations, small group retreats, and one-on-one encounters.

Prior to joining Lead Like Jesus, Phyllis served for eleven years as president of the National Science Center, Inc., in Augusta, Georgia, a partnership with the United States Army, where she collaborated with top military and government officials.

Phyllis's greatest desire is to lead individuals into a deeper relationship with Jesus. Through Lead Like Jesus, she helps equip and empower people around the world to adopt Jesus as their leadership role model so that, through Him, the world will be forever changed.

Phyllis resides in Spartanburg, South Carolina, and enjoys spending time with her four children and nine grandchildren.

INDEX

SCRIPTURE INDEX